THE
ECCENTRIC TEAPOT

THE
ECCENTRIC TEAPOT
FOUR HUNDRED YEARS OF INVENTION

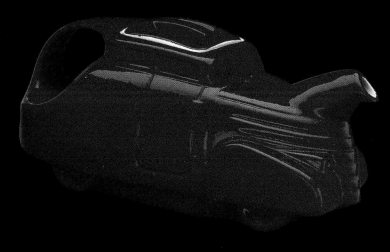

GARTH CLARK

ABBEVILLE PRESS PUBLISHERS NEW YORK

Editor: Constance Herndon
Designer: Julie Rauer
Production Editor: Amy Handy
Production Supervisor: Hope Koturo

Library of Congress Cataloging-in-Publication Data
Clark, Garth, 1947–
     The eccentric teapot: 400 years of invention/
Garth Clark,—1st. ed.
          p.   cm.
     Bibliography: p.
     Includes index.
     ISBN 0-89659-923-X
     1. Teapots—History.   2. Tea.   I. Title.
NK8730.C56   1989
738.2—dc19

Front cover: Martin Bibby, *Bellhop Teapot*, 1985 (See Plate 119).
Back cover, clockwise from upper left: Minton, Ltd., *Cock
and Monkey Teapot*, c. 1880 (See Plate 69). Matheo Thun,
Corvus Corax Teapot, 1982 (See Plate 12). Adrian Saxe,
Gourd Teapot, 1982 (See Plate 132). Jerry Berta, *Diner Tea-
pot*, 1986 (See Plate 82).

Page 1
Minton, Ltd., Britain
Fish Teapot, Majolica ware, c. 1880
Glazed earthenware
7 inches high
Private collection

Page 2
Carol McNicol, Britain
Bird Teapot, 1971
Glazed earthenware
7½ inches high
Collection of Zandra Rhodes

Page 3
Hall China Company, United
States
Car Teapot, c. 1940
Glazed porcelain
5 inches high
Collection of William Strauss

Left:
Cindy Kolodziejski, United States
Sign Language Teapot and Cup,
1987–88
Glazed earthenware, china paint,
luster
8 inches high
Private collection

Page 5
Anthony Bennett, Britain
Garth Clark Editions
Frog/Fossil Teapot, 1983
Glazed earthenware
9 inches high
Private collection

CONTENTS

Plate 1
Britain
Pecten Shell Teapot, Staffordshire
Agate ware, c. 1745
Marbled, colored clays
5 inches high
Sotheby's, New York

Plate 2
Belleek Porcelain Factory, Northern Ireland
Coral Teapot, c. 1875
Glazed porcelain
4¾ inches high
Private collection

In order to prevent the paper-thin porcelain of this teapot from cracking, instructions were printed inside the lid advising the user first to place "blood warm" water in the pot, replacing it with boiling water only when the pot was heated.

Plate 3
Royal Doulton, Britain
Seashell Teapot, Lambeth ware, 1907
Salt-glazed stoneware
5 inches high
Private collection

Plate 4
Amy Sabrina, United States
Autobiographical Teapot, 1987
Glazed earthenware
11 inches high
Private collection

Plate 5
Anne Kraus, United States
*One Day a Dream Was Pointed
Out to Me*, 1986
Glazed earthenware
6¾ inches high
Collection of Betty Asher

———

Kraus's narrative teapot deals with
idealism and hope. Here she depicts a traveler who moves through
the desert, believing, despite the
harsh environment, that a magical
city lies just over the horizon.

Plate 6
Anne Kraus, United States
Shattered Dreams, 1988
Glazed earthenware
6 inches high
Private collection

———

The text on this teapot reads,
"People had warned you against
your ideals, now here you lie dead
in the snow. So now I will carry
this dream until one day I fall and
it shatters once again."

Plate 7
Akio Takamori, United States
Woman Teapot, 1986
Stoneware
6¾ inches high
Collection of Betty Asher

Plate 8
Minton, Ltd., Britain
Man with Mask Teapot,
Majolica ware, c. 1880
Glazed earthenware
5¾ inches high
Private collection

Plate 9
Minton, Ltd., Britain
Man with Sack Teapot,
Majolica ware, c. 1880
Glazed earthenware
5½ inches high
Private collection

Plate 10
Michael Duvall, United States
Untitled, 1987
Glazed earthenware
8½ inches high
Private collection

Plate 11
Peter Shire, United States
Scorpion Teapot, 1984
Glazed earthenware
16¼ inches high
Private collection

Working with the Milan-based Memphis design group, Shire was one of the early proponents of what is now known as Post-Modernism. This piece is an excellent example of his fractured, constructivist style.

Plate 12
Matheo Thun, Italy
Corvus Corax Teapot, 1982
Porcelain
9 inches high
Cooper-Hewitt Museum, New York, the Smithsonian Institution's National Museum of Design

Thun is one of the most prolific of the Memphis designers. This teapot with its barbed handle is an amusing commentary on the relationship of form and function. Its title is the Latin name for raven.

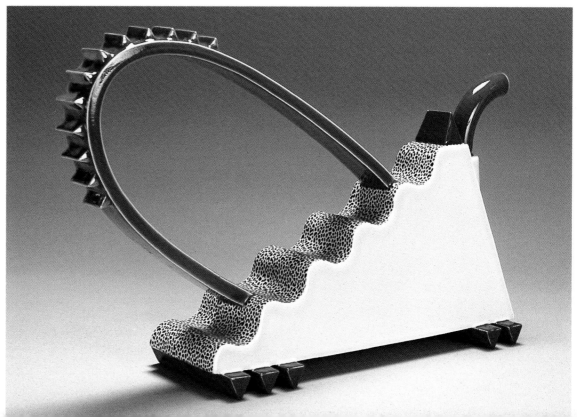

Plate 13
Lingaard Pottery, Britain
*There Was an Old Woman Who
Lived in a Shoe,* 1935
Glazed earthenware
4 inches high
Collection of William Strauss

Plate 14
Lingaard Pottery, Britain
Humpty-Dumpty Teapot, c. 1930
Glazed ceramic
5 inches high
Collection of Karen McCready

Plate 15
Annette Corcoran, United States
Heron Head Teapot, 1987
Porcelain
6½ inches high
Private collection

Plate 16
Luigi Serafini, Italy
Nessy Teapot, 1987
Glazed ceramic
8 inches high
Antonia Jannone Gallery, Milan

Plate 17
Japan
Cat Teapot, c. 1935
Glazed ceramic
5 inches high
Private collection

The Japanese ceramic industry
copied and reinterpreted many of
the English novelty teapots during
the 1930s. This cat teapot was a
particularly successful example.

INTRODUCTION

There is no domestic icon more potent or evocative than the teapot. Its steaming spout fills the air with a reassuring fragrance, promising us that, after a cup or two of its ambrosia, calm will be restored. We reach for the teapot when we want to reward ourselves for a moment of achievement or to take a respite from the day's labors. But we also turn to the teapot at bleaker moments. With its cocky anthropomorphic stance and potbellied gravity, the teapot is the tangible symbol of a life-affirming ritual.

Just as the ceremony of drinking tea is much more than the sum of its parts, so too has the form of the teapot become, in the hands of artists and designers, more than just a receptacle for tea leaves and water. Over the course of centuries the teapot has evolved into a container of unusual ideas, a familiar format for expressing the unfamiliar. Teapots have been created in the shape of birds, fish, cabbages, kings, crowns, camels, and cars. Often it is the tension between these wildly improbable forms and the traditional function of the teapot that inspires the humor, irony, and strange genius of the truly peculiar teapot.

It is to this eccentric edge that this book is dedicated, and to the ability of men and women to transform the everyday into something both

Plate 18
Tea hour: A dowager mother and
her teenage daughters serving tea
on the porch of their New England
home, c. 1900.

Plate 19
Longton Hall, Britain
Cabbage Leaf Teapot, c. 1755
Glazed ceramic
4 inches high
Brian Haughton Antiques, London

delightful and unexpected. Our survey explores a full range of aesthetic and intellectual perspectives, from whimsical visual one-liners to heartfelt political satire, from abstraction to representation. Although some of these teapots do manage to combine an eccentric sensibility with a classic beauty, most have not been created with "good taste" in mind and some do not even serve their function well. But while many are works of art and others are merely clever novelties, all of these teapots share an identity as spouted mavericks far removed from a world of ordered utility. This is no paean to the ordinary teapot; indeed

the preponderance of objects illustrated here would be more at home in the mayhem of the Mad Hatter's tea party than at a stately afternoon tea in the gardens of Buckingham Palace. Their eccentricity celebrates individuality at its most expressive edge, at the point where conventions are overturned and pure originality blossoms.

The teapots selected for this book are a mixture of rare antiques, one-of-a-kind works by artists, and mass-produced industrial objects. Some can still be bought today for very little in a novelty store while others can only be acquired from the finest antique or art dealers. But aristocrat

Plate 20
Michael Frimkess, United States
Alice in Wonderland Teapot,
1975–77
Glazed earthenware, china paint
5 inches high
Collection of Sanford Besser

Plate 21
Gloria Pacosa, United States
Mad Hatter's Tea Party, 1985
Glazed earthenware, mixed media
33 inches high (hare)
Private collection

and commoner mix on these pages with egalitarian ease, and the friendly dialogue that arises between them may transform our ideas of what popular and high culture look like. Although the essays presented here discuss the history of tea ceremonies, teapot design, and tea itself, the gallery of images constitutes a visual history only in the most informal sense. While our teapots are drawn from a period of over four hundred years, contemporary works tend to be featured. Nor are the pots organized chronologically, for such a structure would, in a sense, offend the informal and seditious spirit of the objects themselves. Rather, my selections are personal ones, a group of favorite oddities that, during years of research in the ceramic arts, have struck and held my attention. Assembling them between these covers for a surrealist tea party has been an uncomplicated pleasure that I trust will be shared in the same spirit by the reader.

A BRIEF HISTORY OF TEA

Once the drink of emperors and kings, tea is today the most egalitarian of beverages. This delightful drink is second only to water in worldwide popularity, consumed at a rate of over fifty billion servings a year. Its flavor derives from volatile oils, its astringency from tannin, and its reviving charm from caffeine. Made from the leaves of an evergreen bush that is related to the camellia family, tea provides the body with only four calories, a few B-complex vitamins, and trace minerals.

Of the three thousand varieties of tea most are named in the manner of fine wines, after the region in which they are produced (Assam, Darjeeling, etc.). Once tea reaches the marketplace, however, the regional name is often abandoned in favor of names deriving from leaf size, method of preparation, the person who introduced a particular blend, or caprice—and sometimes combinations of the above. Green, oolong, or black teas, for instance, are not different varieties of tea leaves but rather different processing techniques: green tea is dried without fermenting, oolong is a semifermented tea, and black tea is fully fermented. Orange Pekoe, despite its exotic name, only describes a particular grade of tea—and one of the lowest grades at that. The most popular tea in the United States, it is comprised of small and broken leaf particles.

If the tea drinker is not confused enough, other teas have been given somewhat fanciful names that tell us nothing about flavor or strength. The most misleading of these is Gunpowder tea, the name of which derives from the fact that the leaves are rolled into pelletlike balls that resemble buckshot. Contrary to the expectation inspired by its dramatic name, Gunpowder is a light-hued green tea with a shy, understated taste and the lowest caffeine content of all teas.

Several popular teas have been created by blending teas and then adding flavorings such as herbs or aromatic oils. One of the most successful of these blends was named in 1830 after the second Earl Grey during his brief tenure as prime minister of England. The tea is made primarily from Darjeeling, a large-leafed China tea, mixed with oil from bergamot, a Mediterranean citrus fruit. Constant Comment was also developed as a flavored tea by Mrs. David Bigelow, wife of a noted tea merchant, who perfected this citrus, spice, and tea blend in the kitchen of her Manhattan apartment during the 1940s. Its charming name refers to the conversation at tea time.

There are teas to satisfy (or offend) every taste. The tarry, pungent Lapsang Souchong, not one for the dilettante tea drinker, "is either loved or hated, leaving no room for ambivalence," according to Helen Simpson, author of *The London Ritz Book of Afternoon Tea*. Darjeeling, with its light color and flowery bouquet, is considered the champagne of teas. And Simpson recommends Assam for its malty forthrightness and for delivering what "the British popularly expect from a tea . . . excellent in foul weather."

The amount of caffeine in tea differs from one variety to another. An average cup of black or fermented tea has about a quarter of the caffeine found in a cup of coffee while the same amount of oolong or green tea has even less. Tea lovers claim that coffee and tea also release caffeine differently. Coffee gives up caffeine immediately, creating a jolt of energy, which is then followed by an equally rapid decline, but tea, its devotees insist, releases its caffeine in a gentler, soothing arc.

The remarkable variety of commercially produced teas reflects a rich history that stretches

THÉ.
Thea Sinensis. Rich.

Plate 24
Engraving of the tea bush, some varieties of which produce harvestable leaves and leaf buds for over one hundred years. Plants grow from nine to sixty feet tall. Bronx Botanical Gardens, New York.

Plate 25
The day's harvest goes to the factory at a Ceylon tea plantation. This early nineteenth-century photograph shows an aerial rope railway along which sacks of tea were run to the drying houses.

back four thousand years. The leaf was used in China for its purported medicinal value and only later as a beverage. Although as many tales exist about the creation of the first cup of tea as there are regional varieties of the tea bush, the emperor Shen Neng is credited with being the first tea drinker. Legend has it that the emperor habitually drank only boiled water after he had noticed that those who did so became ill less often. One day on the road (c. 2737 B.C.) he stopped to have his water boiled when a branch from a tea bush accidentally fell into the pot. Shen Neng was entranced both by the fragrant aroma and by the refreshing taste when he drank the water:

the first pot of tea had been prepared.

Another more visceral tale about the beginning of tea sprang from religious lore. In the sixth century the Zen Buddhist patriarch, Bodhidharma, arrived in China from India, and to prove his faith, the tale goes, he decided to meditate for seven years without sleep. After five years, however, Bodhidharma found himself dozing off, so he cut off his eyelids and threw them to ground where they grew into tea bushes—a legend that developed, no doubt, to validate tea drinking by monks struggling to stay awake during long sessions of meditation.

The history of tea preparation, far less veiled

in myth, can be neatly divided into three phases coinciding with the development of boiled tea, powdered tea, and brewed tea. Kakuzo Okakura, in his classic *The Book of Tea*, describes these phases with certain art historical terms, labelling them the Classic, Romantic, and Naturalistic periods of tea. The Classical period started with the beginning of tea drinking and ended in the Tang dynasty (618–907). During this era tea was made from compressed bricks of tea leaves known as tea cakes, which were shredded and boiled with salt into a muddy potion and drunk from a bowl. The Romantic period occurred during the Sung dynasty (960–1280) when a taste developed for a finely powdered tea and tea drinking was first introduced to Japan. Boiling water was poured over the powder, which was then vigorously stirred with a bamboo whisk until the surface was covered by a light foam—a process poetically described by the Chinese as "grinding the fragrant dust and brewing the fresh milky froth."

The Ming dynasty (1368–1644) introduced the Naturalistic period, which has remained with us to the present day. The change came about as a result of the Ming emperor abolishing an unpopular tribute that involved sending tea cakes to the imperial court. Freed from the requirement that they make tea cake for powdered tea, the Chinese turned to brewing tea leaves. This process, which involves steeping the tea in freshly boiled water, required a new addition to the tea service, namely the teapot.

The Ming dynasty also saw radical changes in the cultivation of tea. As traditional tea plantations began to fail they were replaced by modern large-scale farms that employed progressive agricultural techniques. Writing in the sixteenth century, a contemporary observer named Yang Yiqing remarked that the "new plantations are so big that one cannot walk their length in three to five days." The aromatic beverage had inspired a modern industry.

Tea arrived in the West at the beginning of the seventeenth century, first introduced in small quantities by the Portuguese traders. In 1610 the Dutch East India Company began to import tea and became the first tea merchant to the West. (Indeed the Netherlands remains the only country in western continental Europe where tea drinking is still somewhat popular.) England's "Merry Monarch," Charles II, acquired the habit of drinking tea while in exile in The Hague during the English Revolution and introduced to the English court, upon his restoration to the throne, this new and at the time expensive habit. So enamored was Charles of this exotic new libation that when he married the Portuguese princess Catherine of Braganza in 1662, he received as part of her dowry several cases of tea.

Prior to the Restoration, however, during the years of the Cromwellian Protectorate (1653–60), tea had not been looked upon approvingly. In order to win acceptance from the suspicious, pleasure-hating Puritans, the beverage could only be imported if it were described as a medicinal potion. According to a mid-seventeenth-century broadsheet, tea's miraculous properties "helpeth" in the cure of "headaches, giddiness, heaviness, colds, dropsies, scurvies, agues, surfeits and fevers," and it also "expelleth infection." The fears that tea might be banned from England's shores were reasonably founded. The Puritans, as one of their first acts, had made it a crime to bake or eat the Eccles cake, a delightful, currant-filled muffin considered to be "pagan" food. As soon as the Protectorate ended, however, the Eccles cake returned to popularity and later became one of the staples of British afternoon tea.

Although initially prohibitively expensive, tea soon began to appeal to Englishmen of all

Plate 26
China
Teapot, Ming period, c. 1500
Porcelain
4 inches high
Private collection

Despite strenuous attempts to reinvent this simple and effective form, the Ming teapot remains the model for the contemporary teapot.

Plate 27
The Netherlands, which established the tea trade in the seventeenth century, remains the only country in continental Europe where tea drinking is still popular. This Dutch advertisement dates from the late nineteenth century.

classes. After making their employee's tea, servants would reuse leaves to brew their own, and then dry those leaves for resale. The first English tea advertisement appeared on September 30, 1658, in the *Mercurius Politicus*: "That Excellent, and by all Physitians approved *China* drink, called by the *Chineans, Tcha*, by other Nations *Tay alais Tee*, is sold at the Sultaness-Head, a Cophee-House in Sweetings Rents." At this point only men could drink at the Cophee, or coffee, houses. Not until the so-called pleasure gardens were opened during the late eighteenth century in Vauxhall and other London suburbs were women able to drink tea in public. There, anyone with the price of admission could enjoy fireworks and other entertainments and savor a "dish" of tea. (In the eighteenth century tea was served in a dish resembling the Chinese tea bowl. When the handle was added later, the cup as we know it today was introduced.)

By 1689 English companies had begun to import tea directly from China, circumventing the Dutch traders. The fabled tea cutters—fast, sleek-hulled cargo boats—competed for the glory and the profit of bringing in the first teas of the season from China. Within a few years the revenue hungry British government moved to cash in on the burgeoning market for tea and in 1696 the much-hated tea tax was introduced—one shilling on each pound of tea imported by the British East India Company and two shillings and sixpence a pound for other importers.

This move immediately gave rise to tea smuggling and the emergence of a lively black market. Although contraband tea cost five shillings less per pound than the "official" tea, it was frequently adulterated with such additives as sheep droppings, dried hawthorn leaves, and sage. The government then made the selling of impure tea a crime for which one could be imprisoned, so

THE OLD MAID

*The Lady here you see display'd,
By name is still'd an ancient maid,
But if her inward thoughts you'd view,
She thinks herself as young as you,
Oh! Puss forbear to lick the cream,
Your Mistress longs to do the same.*

soon reputable tea dealers began to sell tea in individual bags and guaranteed its quality.

In an attempt to bolster the failing profitability of the British East India Company (which had overstocked the expensive commodity and now had warehouses full of unsold tea), Parliament passed the Tea Act in 1773, the purpose of which was to provide the Company with control over the importation of teas to the British colonies. On December 16 of that year American colonists, enraged by what they perceived as meddling in their affairs, responded with the Boston Tea Party. Dressed as American Indians, the settlers boarded boats in Boston Harbor and tossed their cargoes of tea into the water.

The "tea disorders," as they were known, spread to New York and Annapolis, Maryland, in the next year. They also sparked the first political demonstration by American women when, on October 25, 1774, a group of fifty-one women gathered in Edenton, North Carolina, to sign a petition of protest. A small but appropriate monument to their initiative was erected in the town square, where it still stands today, featuring a revolutionary cannon surmounted by a large, ornamental cast-iron teapot. The British responded to the "tea disorders" with a series of repressive measures, termed the Intolerable Acts by the colonists, which ignited the American Revolution. What had begun literally as a tempest in a teapot developed into a full-blown war of independence.

The British, who had by now become the most insatiable tea drinkers in Europe, repealed the taxes themselves in 1784. Nevertheless tea remained an expensive commodity until the introduction of Indian tea in 1839. In 1823, when it had been discovered that the tea bush was in-

Plate 29
Enraged by British meddling in their affairs, American colonists held a particularly informal tea ceremony known as the Boston Tea Party on December 16, 1773—the first of a series of political protests christened the "tea disorders." This engraving by George Loring Brown represents the colonists, dressed as Native Americans, as they tossed crates of tea into Boston Harbor. The Bostonian Society, Old State House, Boston.

By Special Appointment
To Her Majesty The Queen
Finest the World can produce 1/7 Per Pound.
Largest Sale in the World

LIPTON'S TEAS

One of Lipton's Tea-Gardens CEYLON
From Sunny Ceylon.

Direct from The Gardens
Dambatenne Estates Ceylon · Lipton Tea-Planter Ceylon
Rich, Pure & Fragrant 1/- & 1/4d Per Pound
Appreciated Everywhere
For their Delicious Flavour

CHIEF OFFICES:- CITY ROAD, LONDON.
Branches and Agencies throughout the World.

digenous not only to China but to certain parts of India, the British had proceeded to establish a tea industry there. The first Indian tea was sold at public auction in London in 1839, effectively ending the monopolies that had hitherto controlled and politically manipulated the tea market.

Yet tea did have its detractors among the zealous watchdogs of the Englishman's morality. The writer Henry Sayville denounced tea in 1678 as a "filthy custom," and in 1756 Jonas Hanway claimed, in his *Essay on Tea*, that women could lose their beauty and men their stature

Plate 30
Tea remained a fairly expensive commodity until the introduction of Indian-grown tea in 1839. This 1897 advertisement for Lipton's publicizes the virtues of teas from nearby "sunny Ceylon."

Plate 31
Tea-tasting room in a London packaging factory. This 1935 photograph shows tea tasters checking the uniformity of the firm's blends. About 1500 samples would have been tested in this room each day.

through drinking tea. Even in the nineteenth century, British conservatives were concerned about the debilitating effect of this beverage on the work ethic. In 1822, writing in his book *Cottage Economy*, William Cobbett fulminated against the growing custom of tea drinking by the working class, warning that it must "render the frame feeble, and unfit to encounter hard labour or severe weather, while . . . it deducts from the means of replenishing the belly and covering the back. Hence succeeds a softness, an effeminacy, a seek-

ing for the fire-side, a lurking in bed, and in short, all the characteristics of idleness." In fact, tea drinking in Britain proved to have many positive social benefits for the working class. It encouraged water to be boiled, cutting down the spread of water-borne diseases, and it provided an alternative to the liver-rotting cheap gin, which, until the arrival of tea, had been the favorite drink of many poor people.

During the twentieth century three innovations in tea drinking have been contributed by the United States: iced tea, tea bags, and instant tea—all three viewed as abominations by purists. If Okakura were alive today, he might well have labeled this fourth period of tea the "Pop" period.

Iced tea was actually invented by an Englishman named Richard Blechynden who, unable to sell hot tea at the St. Louis Exposition of 1904, offered tea that had been poured over ice. His iced beverage immediately found favor with the American public, which today consumes three-and-a-half glasses of iced tea for every cup of hot tea.

The tea bag, on the other hand, was devised by Thomas Sullivan, a New York wholesaler who, rather than send tea samples to his clients in small tins, had them sewn into silk bags. To purists, icing tea or steeping it in what are now generally sisal bags qualifies as an affront to the unmediated virtues of the tea leaf. But the American introduction of powdered instant teas in the 1940s, available in a variety of flavors, was seen as the final insult. Americans had demystified the tea ritual and moved the Western ceremony from the parlor to the porch.

Plate 32
Mara Superior, United States
Teapot, 1986
Glazed porcelain
27 inches high
Private collection

Plate 33
Nicholas Homoky, Britain
Untitled, 1983
Inlaid drawing, porcelain
4¾ inches high
Collection of Betty Asher

Homoky reduces the teapot to its
separate elements and "redraws"
it in the abstract.

Plate 34
Roy Lichtenstein, United States
Produced by Rosenthal China, West
Germany
Rosenthal Tea Service, 1984
Glazed porcelain with luster and
on-glaze decoration
7 inches high
Collection of Betty Asher

Pop artist Lichtenstein employs dots
and flat color to portray graphically
the fall of light and shade on the
surface of the teapot.

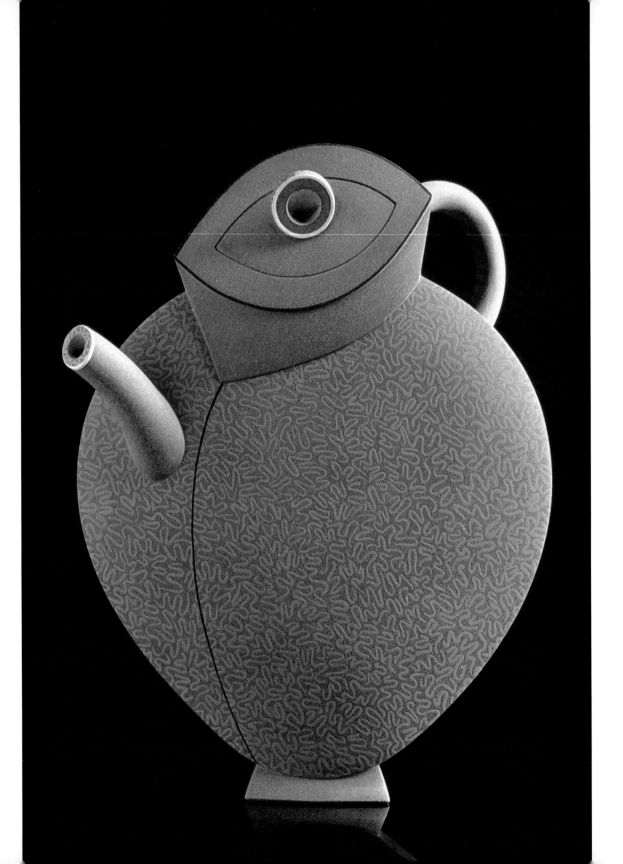

Plate 35
Linda Gunn-Russell, Britain
Untitled, 1985
Glazed earthenware
8¾ inches high
Private collection

Gunn-Russell works in what can
best be termed two-and-a-half
dimensions, using techniques of
drawing and cubist spatial conventions to create flat, graphic teapots.

Plate 36
Harris Deller, United States
Suppressed Teapot, 1986
Incised, glazed porcelain
22 inches high
Private collection

Deller is less concerned with the
teapot as a form than he is with its
potential as a drawing. In this teapot
the form has been "compressed"
rather than "suppressed" into a flat,
graphically powerful shape.

THE RITUALS OF TEA

In both the East and the West tea drinking has long been linked to formal ceremony and highly evolved rituals. In China, where the beverage was first created, tea drinking became closely connected with religion when Buddhist monks began to integrate tea drinking with meditation—an association that lent a strongly spiritual aura to its consumption. "The Philosophy of Tea is not mere aestheticism in the ordinary acceptance of the term," Okakura explains in *The Book of Tea*, "for it expresses conjointly with ethics and religion our whole point of view about man and nature. . . . It represents the true spirit of Eastern democracy by making all its votaries aristocrats in taste."

One of the first known tea masters was an eighth-century Chinese scholar named Lu Wu, author of *Ch'a Ching (The Holy Scripture of Tea)*—quite literally the bible of the Chinese tea connoisseur. Lu Wu presented tea as an act of domestic poetry in which every aspect of its appreciation was elevated to an art form, from the required appearance of tea leaves to the manner in which tea was served. He insisted that the best leaves must "crease like the leathern boot of Tartar horsemen, curl like the dewlap of a mighty bullock, unfold like mist rising out of a ravine, gleam like a lake touched by a zephyr, and be

Plate 37
Afternoon tea in a garden near Clivedon by the Thames River in Britain, c. 1895.

Plate 38
Britain
Coronation Teapot, 1910
Glazed earthenware
5 inches high
Private collection

wet and soft like fine earth newly swept by rain."

Tea connoisseurship reached new heights during the Sung dynasty when powdered tea was introduced and salt was discarded from its preparation. The informed discussion of tea and a knowledge of its many varieties was considered an essential part of one's education and refinement. Okakura quotes a Sung poet who listed the three most deplorable things in the world as "the spoiling of fine youths through false education, the degradation of fine paintings through vulgar admiration and the utter waste of fine tea through incompetent manipulation." At all levels of Chinese society, "tea contests" were held to taste and judge tea. These ceremonies evolved into elaborate and sumptuous feasts where the most ostentatious displays of wealth were encouraged.

The Japanese eventually rescued tea from this decadent condition and in the fifteenth century brought the tea ceremony to its spiritual apex. The practice of drinking powdered green tea had first been introduced to Japan in the twelfth century by monks returning from study at the Zen monasteries of China. While the monks valued it as a tool to propagate Zen, tea drinking among the wealthy became an excuse for staging tea parties as lavish as those in China. These noisy affairs featured gambling, public bathing, liberal quantities of sake, massive meals, and an ostentatious display of expensive tea utensils that were imported from China.

Towards the end of the fifteenth century, however, a Zen priest named Murato Shuka (1422–1503), began a serious study of tea and its rituals. Shuka positioned tea drinking within the context of Zen, which holds that every act of daily life can lead to enlightenment. He began to refine the manner in which tea was presented, doing away with the excesses and the imported

Chinese treasures. And he preferred the quality of the cruder Japanese tea utensils, seeing beauty in imperfection. "More than a full moon shining brightly on a clear night," Shuka is quoted as saying, "I prefer to see a moon that is partially hidden by clouds." His example began to be emulated by a number of tea drinkers from the merchant class, a group that developed a secular tea philosophy known as *Chado*, or "the Way of Tea." Out of their midst emerged Japan's first tea master, Takeno Jo-O (1502–55), who introduced the tea ceremony or *cha-no-yu* (literally, "hot water for tea"), a celebration of the humble and the ordinary.

However Jo-O's apprentice Sen Rikyu (1522–91) is credited with refining the ceremony and establishing its four principles; harmony, respect, purity, and tranquility. Rikyu required that *cha-no-yu* be performed in a separate teahouse built with common materials to suggest humility and poverty. These tiny structures were nevertheless built with such exacting craftsmanship and attention to design that, paradoxically, they were extremely costly to erect.

These private teahouses were the highest expression of the elusive aesthetic character of the tea ceremony known as *wabi*. In its most direct translation *wabi* means rusticity. But, more than a search for rustic simplicity, *wabi* suggests a complex state of mind in which the tea master attempts, through his actions, the choice of tea implements, and the level of discussion, to achieve a tranquil, contemplative state of frugality and humility.

Rikyu's teachings contributed significantly to the extraordinary flowering of the humanities that took place in Japan during the Momoyama period (1573–1615). His considerable aesthetic influence came to an abrupt end, however, when his all-powerful protector, Taiko Hideyoshi, invited

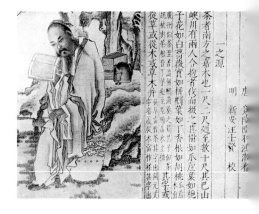

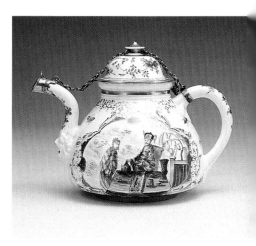

Plate 40
Meissen Porcelain Works, Germany
Teapot and Cover, 1723
Porcelain and silver
4¾ inches high
Courtesy of Sotheby's, New York

The scene on this teapot is attributed to the famous court painter, Johann Gregor Horolt, and shows a Chinese nobleman taking tea.

him to commit ritual suicide in response to ru-
mors that Rikyu had been conspiring to poison
the despot. Rikyu administered the tea ceremony
for the last time and at its conclusion, in the presence of his closest friend, took his life. "The Last

Tea of Rikyu," wrote Okakura, "will stand forth
forever as the acme of tragic grandeur."

Nothing could be further apart than the
tea ceremonies of Japan and England. English
tea became an event as hedonistic as its Japan-

A little friendly gossip, a social cup of Tea, and when the tea was Twining's who happier could be?

ese counterpart was pared down and monastic. While the essential elements were much the same—carefully selected tea implements, strictly observed etiquette, exaggerated politeness, careful dress for the occasion, delightful sweets to tempt the palate, and beautifully arranged vases of flowers to please the eye—no sense of *wabi* was evident at these crowded soirees. The very notion that a Mayfair hostess should attempt to achieve "rustic simplicity" was unthinkable, a contradiction of the lavish spirit of the British afternoon tea.

By the beginning of the nineteenth century, tea had become fully entrenched in British society. Indeed a young Swede visiting England in 1809 remarked that "next to water, tea is the Englishman's proper element." Yet tea drinking was still a relatively informal activity at that time and it was not until 1840, two hundred years after the first teas were imported to England, that the ceremony of afternoon tea emerged. The seventh Duchess of Bedford had developed the habit of having a pot of tea and some cake or buttered bread sent up to her room around four o'clock to overcome late afternoon listlessness. When she invited her friends to join her an institution was born.

The ceremony soon grew more and more lavish as each hostess attempted to outdo the hospitality of her peers. Before long tea was being chased down with heady orange liqueurs or claret punches, and tables groaned with calorie-laden delectables. While musicians played, tea was poured from elaborate silver teapots into expensive china and then served by liveried footmen to elegant women in diaphanous, loose-waisted tea gowns. Conversation could indeed be lively, but rather than focusing on art and philosophy, tea chatter was usually given over to witty banter or an exchange of the day's most salacious gossip. The British tea ceremony, in comparison to the minimalism of *cha-no-yu*, was a deliciously decadent event.

The belle époque of afternoon tea was

Plate 43
Somber Victorian family at tea,
c. 1865.

several cakes, soft drinks, and a claret cup. A complex etiquette arose and books filled with anxious advice alerted tea drinkers to the finer points of behavior. "Those who take sugar with their tea are advised to propel the spoon with a minimum of effort," one author warned, "and to remove it without fail before raising the cup."

For all its excesses, afternoon tea was nonetheless a strictly codified ritual administered with a genuine passion and respect for tea. The British tea ceremony even won praise from the discerning Okakura. "In the delicate clatter of trays and saucers," he wrote, "in the soft rustle of feminine hospitality, in the common catechism about cream and sugar, we know that the Worship of Tea is established beyond question." Henry James concurred in the opening paragraph of *The Portrait of a Lady*, remarking that "there are few hours in life more agreeable than the hour dedicated to the ceremony of afternoon tea"—even, he added, if one did not drink tea.

In addition to the elegant afternoon tea, a number of tea "ceremonies" arose in Britain. High tea, which, contrary to its name, was not an elegant tea at all, developed as a stoic farmhouse meal. Served at six o'clock in the evening, it offered more of a supper than a tea, featuring pork pies, scotch eggs, and other substantial foods. Tea would be poured out of a simple firestone teapot in a brew strong enough, in the worker's patois, "to trot a mouse on." Somewhat scaled down, a version of high tea still survives today in parts of northern England and in Scotland.

In the nineteenth century students at boarding schools and universities created their own daily tea rituals by toasting bread and crumpets at the fireplace in their rooms. At men's clubs a hearty tea was served that included substantial sandwiches and savory snacks such as potted shrimp, deviled ham toasts, and scotch wood-

reached at the beginning of the twentieth century, when a typical menu for formal tea might include tea, coffee (for heretics), bread and butter, five kinds of sandwiches, oyster *vol au vents*, chicken cutlets, two creams, four jellies, an ice,

cock (a mixture of anchovies, cream, and egg served on hot toast). For the working class, on the other hand, tea was more Spartan and usually included little more than a mug of sweetened tea, bread, or a few tea biscuits.

Yet for the laborer as much as for the duke the tea ceremony provided a momentary truce from the mayhem of life. For an hour or two the class war was halted. So too was the war of the sexes, for tea was a time for meeting friends, not lovers. Tea's gentle euphoria provided a sense of well-being that enabled Englishmen from all walks of life to face whatever tasks remained for the rest of the day. Teatime was a moment to reflect, to replenish hope, and to daydream a little. In the most egalitarian and non-denominational sense it was a deeply religious moment, savored and celebrated daily by an entire nation.

Afternoon tea was made accessible to all classes by the arrival of tea shops in the mid-nineteenth century. The first was opened by the Aerated Baking Company (ABC) in 1864 and, proving to be immensely popular, others spread across England. Tearooms soon appeared throughout the British empire. There was no greater treat for a child than to be taken to one of these temples of confectionary, with its tempting array of iced buns, cream cakes, and dainty petit fours.

After the First World War tea began to lose its grandeur but not its importance. While hotels such as London's Ritz still provided large formal teas, society's changing values, rhythms, and priorities meant that tea at home became a much more intimate event, scaled down for the family or the closest of friends. This shift in emphasis was reflected in the popularity during the 1920s of the so-called tête-à-tête tea services for two. Growing health and fashion consciousness also resulted in a trimming back of the menu to its original fare—a few tea sandwiches and a modest slice of cake.

Plate 44
Afternoon tea taken by three ladies in the garden of a fashionable American home, c. 1905.

IT WAS AN OFFER SHE
DARE NOT REFUSE

Plate 45
Despite the implications of this 1978 Glen Baxter cartoon, tea time was not an occassion for sexual aggression. Gentle courting was allowed but tea was a moment when the war between the sexes gave way to the gentler rhythms of friendship.

In the 1930s the tea ceremony took on a new form with the introduction of the tea dance, during which one could enjoy a cup of tea and dance to the big bands of the day. But the hectic modern world has slowly eroded our leisure time and transformed afternoon tea into an occasional indulgence rather than a daily ritual. After the Second World War the tearoom began to lose favor. Most of London's ABC shops have now returned to their original forms as bakeries, retaining a few dispirited side tables at which to grab a cup of greasy stewed tea and a bland pastry.

While British tea has lost much of its ceremonial form and the attendant sense of theater, there is still no other place in the Western world where a cup of perfectly brewed tea is more revered. Splendid tea is still served in the Palm Court of the Ritz in London while a less elegant but acceptable version, if one can tolerate the crowds, can be taken at the tearooms of Fortnum and Mason's or Liberty's. Outside of London one can nevertheless still encounter sumptuous teas at country inns and village tearooms that have obstinately held out against the times.

America, despite its Anglophilic disposition, never has taken to tea with the same enthusiasm as Britain. Writing in *The Tea Lover's Treasury*, James Norwood Pratt suggests that "amidst the roar of canon and musketry . . . the Great Republic was born with a pre-natal disinclination for tea." While tea and patriotism did make unhappy bedfellows during the founding of the Republic, tea remained an important part of social life in Boston, New York, and certain others parts of eastern and southern America. The Prince de Broglie, visiting America in 1892, remarked that he possessed all the elements of success in this new society because, although he understood only a few words of English, he "knew better how to drink excellent tea with even better cream, how

to tell a lady she was pretty and a gentleman he was sensible." Another visitor in the late eighteenth century, Comte de Segur, noted that his health continued to be excellent "despite the quantity of tea one must drink with the ladies out of gallantry and of madeira all day long with the men out of politeness."

By the mid-nineteenth century, however, tea had begun to lose its favor as the country's fancy turned to coffee. Although America is now the second largest importer of tea, its per capita consumption is less than one-tenth that of Britain and Ireland. And yet America, the home of instant tea, is now leading something of a revival of the formal afternoon tea. In the major cities increasing numbers of restaurants and hotels are introducing elegant teas replete with clotted cream and scones, sandwiches, cakes, and several varieties of tea. As more business executives are choosing to meet over afternoon tea instead of lunch, we find ourselves poised on the brink of a new yuppie era, that of the "power" tea.

Plate 46
Delft, Netherlands
Teapot and Brazier, c. 1880
Tin-glazed earthenware
14 inches high
The Metropolitan Museum of Art,
New York, gift of Henry C. Marquand

Plate 47
George E. Ohr, United States
Untitled, c. 1900
Glazed earthenware
9 inches high
Collection of Jederman, N.A.

Maverick potter George Ohr produced pieces that were marvels of manipulation. His "clay babies," as he termed them, were thrown on the wheel and altered into sensually anthropomorphic shapes of which there were "no two pots alike."

Plate 48
Meissen Porcelain Works, Germany
Cadogan Teapot, c. 1725
Glazed porcelain with on-glaze
decoration
5¾ inches high
The Metropolitan Museum of Art,
New York, bequest of Emma A.
Schaefer, 1974, the Lesley and
Emma Schaefer Collection

The Cadogan, modeled on the Chinese wine pot, is filled through a
hole in the base with strained, already brewed tea. A special plumbing system prevents the tea from
leaking out when the teapot is
placed upright.

Plate 49
James Lawton, United States
Red Scalloped Teapot, 1985
Raku
7 inches high
Private collection

Lawton has fired this teapot according to the fifteenth-century Japanese tradition of raku, which involves glazing the surface of the pot during a brief, fierce firing that lasts only a few minutes

Plate 50
Paul Mathieu, Canada
Untitled, 1984
Glazed porcelain
6¼ inches high
Collection of Betty Asher

This teapot explores the contradiction between the hard, tough surface of the glazed porcelain and the soft, quilted form it evokes.

Plate 51
Mike Johns, United States
Rock Teapot, 1987
Earthenware, glaze, luster
12 inches high
Private collection

Art and nature collide and merge in this playful assembly of rocklike forms decorated with a lively surface of luster and china paint.

Plate 52
Ralph Bacerra, United States
Garth Clark Editions
Pyramidal Teapot, 1984
Glazed earthenware
14¼ inches high
Collection of Betty Asher

This teapot, an elegant play with geometry, takes the form of an inverted pyramid held upright on a small base. One of a series of eight teapots, each of which was decorated with a different surface, this piece required up to five firings to create its rich layered surface.

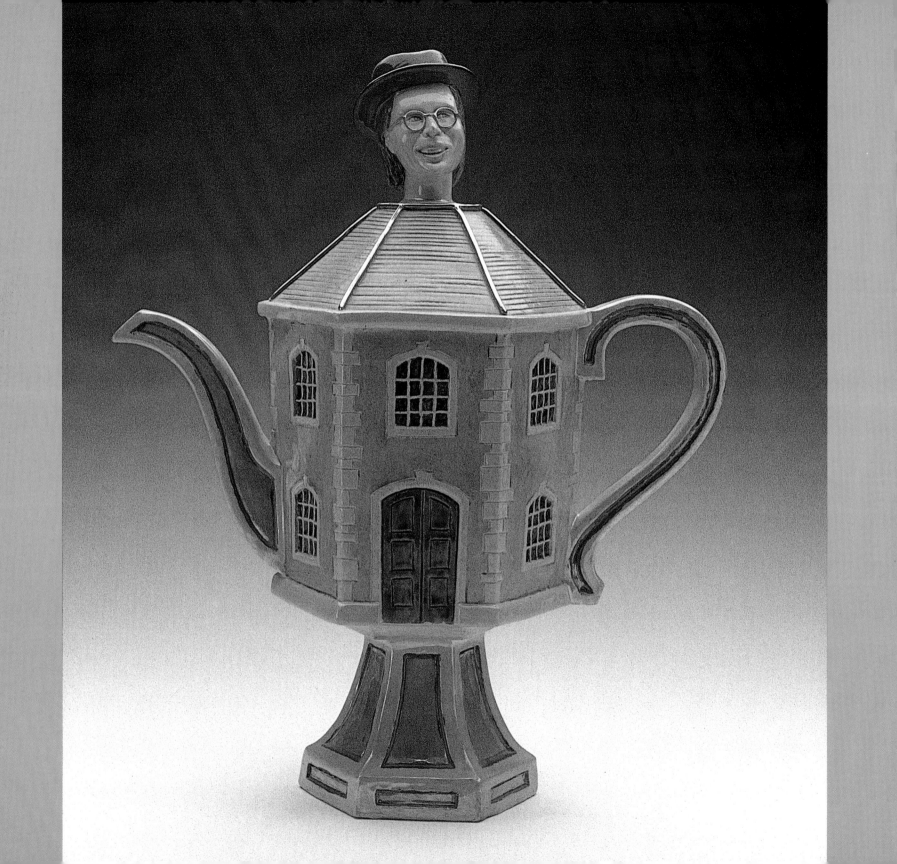

THE TEAPOT

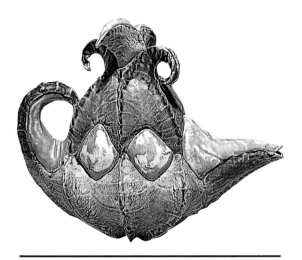

A crucial aesthetic element of the tea ceremony, whether in China, Japan, or England, is the selection of the utensils used for making and serving tea. Before the development of the teapot during the Ming dynasty the most important item of tea-ware was the bowl in which tea was both prepared and served. Blue glazed bowls were considered the perfect choice during the Tang dynasty because their color altered the appearance of the boiled tea from an unpalatable pink to a jade green. The rise of powdered teas during the Sung dynasty inspired a different palette that emphasized the dark, streaked glazes known as "hare's fur" as the suitable complement to the muddy gray-green liquid. Brewed teas favored white glazed porcelain cups to highlight the range of tea colors from light greens to rich saffron and amber.

But it was the Japanese *cha-no-yu* that had the greatest impact on the developing aesthetic of tea utensils. Inspired by the tea masters, a generation of masterful potters arose including Chōjirō, the father of the rough, dark earthenware called raku, and Ogata Kenzan, a producer of masterfully decorated wares. These potters were revered and their bowls and dishes were consid-

Plate 53
Andrew Wood, Britain
Self-Portrait Teapot, 1980
Glazed earthenware
10¾ inches high
Collection of Betty Asher

Wood has employed a model of
the building that houses his pottery
as the main form for this amusing
self-portrait.

Plate 54
Kim Dickey, United States
Heartsease Teapot, 1988
Porcelain
6 inches high
Collection of Daniel Jacobs

ered high art. Kenzan and others established pottery dynasties that continue to this day to work in the spirit and style of the early masters.

The impact of *cha-no-yu* extended far beyond ceramics, however: it also set standards for landscaping, established classic patterns for textiles, refined the art of flower arranging, and profoundly influenced Japanese architecture. Unfortunately this creative largesse did not extend to the design of the teapot when it was introduced. Even today *cha-no-yu* has maintained the Sung custom of whisking powdered tea in a bowl. Eventually the teapot did find popular usage in Japan but only outside the walls of the ritual teahouse.

In China, however, the development of the teapot resulted in a period of extraordinary invention. The most significant of the early teapots were produced from 1510 onwards in the Yixing region, an area renowned for thousands of years as the pottery capital of China. Yixing's fame derives in part from the discovery of local deposits of an exceptionally refined stoneware clay. According to Chinese mythology the clay was revealed by a strange monk who appeared one day in a village. "Riches and honors for sale!" he called out, but villagers laughed at him. "If you will not buy honors, then what about riches?" he insisted. Leading the villagers to a nearby cave he instructed them to dig, revealing a seam of clay with five colors each as brilliant as brocade.

With a texture of satin and a color ranging from light buff to rich purplish brown, the Yixing clays are indeed remarkable—so much so that some potters chose not to glaze their pots at all. Preferring to exploit the natural beauty and tactility of the clay they often left the surface bare, sometimes enhancing it by buffing it to a high gloss on the lapidary wheel. The earliest Yixing teapots were made by carving the main form from a solid piece of clay with a bamboo knife. Handles and a spout were added later. Around 1580 a new technique emerged that involved modeling the teapot by hand and then turning it to the desired shape on a wheel. By the eighteenth century, however, teapots had become so popular that new methods had to be adopted to increase production. The potters began to cast teapots in sectional molds, assembling the pieces and finishing the forms by hand—the technique still used in Yixing production today.

Despite the elegance and sophisticated design of the Yixing teapots, only glazed porcelain was considered of sufficiently high quality for the imperial court. Instead Yixing wares attracted scholars and poets who, in the late eighteenth century, began to involve themselves in their design and production. The role of intellectuals in the evolution of the Yixing teapot is a complex and fascinating one. Some poets or writers inscribed poems on teapots. Others selected appropriate clays, influenced the method of construction, or determined the size and proportions of a particular teapot. In this cerebral environment every element of a teapot was discussed, critiqued, and often, improved upon. "This connection between scholars and I-hsing ware was probably responsible for raising the stature of the ware from that of utilitarian objects to that of works of art," Therese Tse Bartholomew suggested in her essay, *I-hsing Wares.* "Such collaboration between scholars and craftsmen has seldom been seen in the history of Chinese art." The fascination of the literati with the teapot encouraged potters to push their aesthetic goals beyond merely meeting the simple design requirements of making a visually satisfying object and instead marked the point at which the teapot became a format for artistic self-expression.

In addition to using reductive, classical forms,

Plate 55
Josiah Wedgwood and Sons, Ltd.,
Britain
The Veilleuse, c. 1795
Creamware
12 inches high
Private collection

This unit consists of a teapot that sits on a stand in which a bowl of water can be kept warm by a small lamp. The water is used to dilute the second cup of tea.

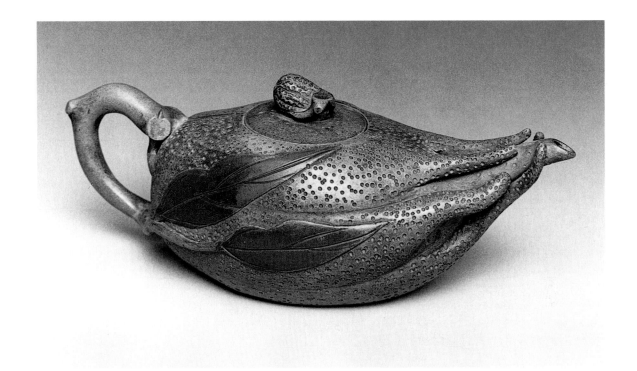

Plate 56
China
Teapot, Yixing ware, nineteenth century
Stoneware
3¾ inches high
Nelson-Atkins Museum of Art, Kansas City

The shape of this teapot derives from a fruit known to the Chinese as "Buddha Fingers."

the Yixing potter also embellished his pots with a vocabulary drawn from everyday life and nature. While some of these stylizations were simply imaginative, others had auspicious meanings in Chinese culture. A peach-shaped form conveyed wishes for longevity and good luck, for instance, while a pomegranate shape encrusted with naturalistic fruit and nuts offered the promise of numerous healthy offspring (Plate 122).

Yixing teapots were the first to be imported by the West and their two styles—classicism and inventive naturalism—therefore had a profound impact on Western ceramic design. These extensively imitated pieces inspired the development of unglazed stoneware by pioneer potters such as Johann Friedrich Bottger. Thomas Astbury, Ralph Wood, and Josiah Wedgwood.

Many porcelain factories in Europe produced teapots during the early eighteenth century. The services created at Meissen in Germany and Sèvres in France are of particular interest for their gilded, enameled, over-wrought ostentation (Plates 40, 48, 70, 77, 113). However continental Europe preferred coffee and chocolate to tea and consequently the exploration of teapot forms was never carried to the same level of obsession as it was in England. From 1750 onwards this small island dominated the art of creating teapots.

Josiah Wedgwood (1730–95), England's so-called potter to the world, encouraged the rapid spread of tea drinking in the West by perfecting the industrial mass production of a resilient pottery known as creamware (Plates 55, 57). In 1765 Queen Charlotte ordered a service of this white Devonshire clay under a clear glaze and was so pleased with Wedgwood's product that she had it named Queen's Ware. Wedgwood expanded production rapidly and soon handsomely potted teapots and cups were affordable to all but the very poor.

Wedgwood, whose taste was essentially classical and conservative, produced only one body of work that is of interest to this study of unusual teapots. In 1759, while in partnership with Thomas Whieldon, the twenty-nine-year-old Wedgwood developed a series of distinctive teapots in the form of cauliflowers, pineapples, and cabbages with finely molded spouts and crabstock handles (Plates 57, 130, 131). Although other potteries, notably Longton Hall (Plate 19), produced works in this botanical genre that were artistically finer, Wedgwood's teapots were the most superbly potted of the day. The Whieldon/Wedgwood pieces are a joy to hold: delicately walled, light as a feather, perfectly balanced, and with a characteristic attention to such details as removing seams from the molding process.

The mid-eighteenth century was a period of extraordinary invention in the British ceramics industry. Sensual Agate ware teapots made from a variety of colored clays (Plate 1) vied with the sleek surfaces of the Staffordshire salt-glazed teapots, one of the finest examples of which was produced around 1755 (Plate 58). Its cleverly stylized decoration derived from the fossil shapes found in limestone strata, and though the design is over three hundred years old it remains as contemporary as any twentieth-century pattern.

The first three-quarters of the nineteenth century was a period of excessive, muddled eclecticism characterized by revivalist styles. The palpable aesthetic deficiencies of the era were apparent in 1851 at London's Great Exhibition held in the Crystal Palace. The mediocrity of the decorative arts displayed there so mortified those with more discerning tastes that it set off a series

of reformist movements. Sir Henry Cole led an "Art and Industry" campaign that resulted in, among other things, the foundation of the Royal College of Art and the Victoria and Albert Museum. But Cole's interest in design reform predated the Great Exhibition. In 1846 he had decided to demonstrate his design principles with a sober, portly, if not particularly imaginative, teapot, which he entered in a design competition under the pseudonym of Felix Summerly. This piece won the silver medal from the Society of Arts (Plate 60).

At the opposite pole from Cole's vision of a pragmatic marriage between art and industry stood the Aesthetic Movement, an anti-industrial, art-for-art's-sake school that later evolved into the Arts and Crafts Movement. Their approach was spoofed in 1880–81 by a Worcester Porcelain Company teapot satirizing Oscar Wilde, one of the leading lights of the Aesthetic Movement (Plate 102).

This teapot was inspired by a remark that Wilde made in 1875 while still a student at Oxford University. Wilde had just acquired two blue china vases for his rooms and declared, "I find it harder and harder every day to live up to my blue china." This memorable epigram provided Wilde with instant notoriety. It is difficult to understand today why the British found his remark so outrageous, but even the Anglican church was drawn into the fray. According to one angry Anglican priest Wilde's remark constituted "a form of heathenism which it is our bounden duty to fight against and crush out, if possible." Five years later *Punch* magazine carried a series of caricatures by George Du Maurier representing Wilde as the archetypal aesthete, "Ossian Wilderness." The drawings made fun of Wilde's flowing locks, his blue china, and his penchant for white lilies.

The Worcester teapot (or rather teapots, for

Plate 57
Whieldon/Wedgwood, Britain
Cauliflower Teapot, c. 1765
Creamware
5 inches high
Everson Museum of Art, Syracuse, New York

Plate 58
Britain
Fossil Teapot, Staffordshire ware, c. 1755
Salt-glazed stoneware
4 inches high
Nelson-Atkins Museum of Art, Kansas City

Although this design is over two hundred years old it still conveys a startling sense of modernity. Its dramatic motif is drawn from the fossil shapes in limestone strata.

Plate 59
Maurice Dufrêne, France
Teapot, 1904
Porcelain
8 inches high
Private collection

In this design for a boutique in Paris called La Maison Moderne, Dufrêne sought to mirror in both form and decoration the liquid "pouring" function of the teapot itself.

Plate 60
Felix Summerly (Henry Cole), Britain
Produced by Minton Ltd., Britain
Teapot, 1846
Porcelain
5¾ inches high
Victoria and Albert Museum, London

two slightly different versions were produced) presumably took its cue from *Punch*'s caricatures. On one side it depicts Wilde foppishly posing with a huge sunflower buttonhole. One hand rests on his hip to create the handle while the other limply defines the spout. The other side of the teapot shows him as a young woman with a white lily across her breast. On the base is inscribed, "Fearful consequences through the laws of natural selection and evolution of living up to one's teapot."

The satire was meant to be malicious, a cruel suggestion of the Aesthetic Movement's effeminacy raised by Britain's moralists, who were ever alert for attacks on what one must assume was their fragile sense of manhood. Yet this teapot's sexual ambiguity, its languid sense of style, and its campiness do in fact capture much of the self-consciousness, complexity, and sensuality of the Aesthetic Movement. And its sensitive modeling, subtle glazing, and powerful characterization make it a minor masterpiece of late nineteenth-century decorative art.

Spurred on by the atmosphere of reform, art and design moved rapidly ahead. As part of Minton's popular and much-imitated Majolica ware, the firm created a masterful series of teapots in 1874 comprised of colorful gourds, monkeys holding onto melons, fish pierced with bamboo spouts, and Chinese men in various poses (p. 1 and Plates 8, 9, 69, 78, 126). The modeling on these teapots is tightly integrated and superbly realized (if one can ignore the frequently sadistic placement of the handles and spouts). The inspiration for the Majolica wares came from several sources ranging from Yixing teapots to Japanese art. But the greatest influence came from the works of the French Mannerist, Bernard Palissy, whose wares established the palette and liquid, polychromatic mood of these

works. Majolica ware's use of plant and animal forms was a continuation of eighteenth-century ceramic traditions, adjusted to suit the Victorian sensibility.

As the century came to a close, design took yet another turn with the rise of Art Nouveau. Plant motifs, popular in the ceramics of both the eighteenth and nineteenth centuries, were now taken a step further and abstracted into whiplash lines and sensual, undulating organic forms. Henry van de Velde, Maurice Dufrêne (Plate 59), and others created elegant teapots that beautifully expressed the linear thrall of Art Nouveau. Jugendstil, its Germanic version, imparted a more rational, geometric objectivity to the style.

If we examine the eccentric edge of Art Nouveau—or rather the *more* eccentric edge —the teapots of Holland's Rozenburg Plateelfabriek hold the greatest interest (Plate 127). In 1899 Rozenburg introduced a line of paper-thin wares known as eggshell porcelains (although the clay body was actually a refined white earthenware). Designed by the factory's director, J. Jurriaan Kok, the teapots were a curious mixture of theatrical form, with their distinctive, pierced "Pixie cap" lids, and delicate, almost naturalistically painted floral decoration.

With their curious contrariness between surface and form, these are by no means the most resolved of the Art Nouveau designs. But they are among the most imaginative and ambitious objects of their day, with their ethereal paintings of flowers, plants, birds, and insects, and their gossamer lightness, which creates a dreamlike evocation of the teapot.

The fin de siècle was a period of remarkable aesthetic invention and one that launched a determined assault on the functional simplicity of the teapot. One of the earliest of these curiosities was the lidless Cadogan teapot, which was first produced in the 1700s (Plate 48) and enjoyed revived popularity in the nineteenth century. Based on the shape of the Chinese wine pot, the Cadogan had a clever internal plumbing system whereby already brewed tea was poured in through a hole in the base of the teapot. In 1860 Wedgwood also produced an endogynous, multipart teapot/coffeepot, a complex device that the American potter George E. Ohr gave an amusing twist to in his 1900 version of this unhappy marriage (Plate 61).

In the late 1890s a self-pouring teapot was developed with a pump built into the lid so that the hostess did not have to lift the pot to pour.

Not a particularly elegant device, it made its users look as though they were dispensing draught beer in a pub. The problem of "stewed" tea, which had been steeped for too long and had absorbed an unpleasant level of tannin, was also addressed during these years. The Earl of Dundonald's S.Y.P. teapot (Simple Yet Perfect) from 1907 was created with two separate compartments (Plate 63). The tea was brewed in the first while the teapot lay on its back; after three to five minutes it was set upright and the tea flowed through a strainer into the second chamber *sans* tea leaves. The S.Y.P. was an effective innovation but it never caught on with the tea drinking public and production was discontinued in 1921.

The first electric automatic teapot was invented in 1909, an innovation that has never had the appeal of its coffee counterpart. The cube teapot, patented in 1916 by R. C. Johnson, was extensively used on the Cunard Line during the 1930s because of the far greater stability its square shape afforded (Plate 62). Few of these innovations survived for more than a decade or two, however, and contemporary attempts, such as handleless, double-walled teapots from Denmark's Bing and Grohndal, have fared poorly as well. With the exception of minor design adjustments such as the addition of an internal leaf strainer, the functional perfection of the Ming dynasty teapot remains unchallenged as the model for the teapots that we use today.

Aesthetic invention, however, continued to thrive. As the first half of the century produced extraordinary developments in modern art, design, and architecture, so too did the ceramic art movement develop parallel momentum. Potters began to seek the same creative autonomy and status as the fine artists, and painters and sculptors likewise began to involve themselves in the so-called minor arts, designing furniture

Plate 61
George E. Ohr, United States
Coffeepot/Teapot, c. 1900
Glazed earthenware
12 inches high
Collection of the Smithsonian Institution, Washington, D.C.

Ohr enjoyed playing games with utility, making trickily contorted cups he called puzzle mugs as well as other "gimcracks." This unlikely combination of a teapot and coffeepot is glazed in a gun-metal gray on one side and in a speckled green on the other.

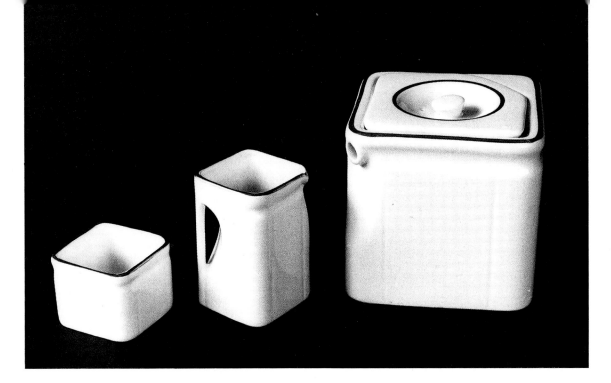

The cube teapot found favor with
the Cunard Steamship Line, making up in stability and storability
for its tendency to dribble tea from
its almost vestigal spout.

The S.Y.P. teapot (for Simple Yet
Perfect) brews tea in one position
(above) and is then placed on its
foot so that the tea drains through
a sieve into a separate container
from which it can be poured.

and other household objects.

One of the most important modern teapots
to emerge from the fine arts world was designed
around 1920 by Kasemir Malevich, the founder
of the Suprematist movement (Plate 64). An awk-
ward but brutally powerful assemblage of volumes,
the piece was criticized on functional grounds by
the director of the Leningrad State Porcelain
Works. Malevich responded that this was not a
teapot at all, but the *idea* of a teapot—a remark
that exemplified the extent to which ceramic artists had begun to see their involvement with functionalism as an increasingly symbolic relationship.

The ceramics community itself was strongly
divided on the issue of functionalism. Many agreed
with Malevich's contention that handmade pots
should be created to satisfy intellectual and emotional needs, not utilitarian ones. In an industrial
age, they argued, there is no sense in trying to
compete with a massive ceramics industry. Others, however, took a harder and more traditional
line. Inspired by potters such as Bernard Leach,
Michael Cardew, Harry Davis, and Warren Mac-
Kenzie, many insisted that utility was the source
of aesthetic beauty and viewed any eccentric
expression as inexcusable self-indulgence.

While twentieth-century potters differed
strongly on issues of functionalism, both camps
agreed that the teapot was one of pottery's most
challenging forms. "The balance of the spout and
handle of a teapot, with each other and with the
body of the pot, is an aesthetic problem to which
no artist need be ashamed to devote his attention," wrote the distinguished art historian, Sir
Herbert Read, in his book *Art and Industry* in
1936. "There is not only the problem of balanc-
ing two linear forms, each with a distinct function, against each other, but these forms must
both accord with the three dimensional volume
of the body of the pot. The correct solution of
this problem is one of the rarest of aesthetic
achievements."

From Malevich's Suprematist vessels to Salvador Dali's and Roy Lichtenstein's designs for Rosenthal China, many non-ceramic artists have been tempted to wrestle with the design challenge of the teapot. Likewise some of the best-known architects of our time have risen to the challenge, among them Henry van de Velde, Frank Lloyd Wright, Peter Behrens, Josef Hoffmann, Walter Gropius, Michael Graves, Stanley Tygerman (Plate 84), and Robert Venturi.

The earliest body of American "art" teapots, and certainly one of the most eccentric, come from a maverick potter in Biloxi, Mississippi, named George Edgar Ohr (1857–1918). Ohr was obsessed with the wheel, to which he responded, according to his own description, "like a wild duck in water," throwing vessels of extraordinary thinness. These he manipulated into bizarre configurations, denting, crinkling, distorting, folding, ruffling, and tearing his forms into exciting, highly articulated shapes (Plates 48, 61).

Apart from the occasional industrially made

Plate 64
Kasemir Malevich, Russia
Produced by the Leningrad State
Porcelain Works
Suprematist Teapot and Cup,
c. 1920

With these revolutionary objects Malevich sought to express the *idea* of a cup or a teapot rather than address their purpose.

Plate 65
Robert Arneson, United States
*A Social Gathering for the Late
Afternoon,* 1969
Glazed earthenware
12 inches high
Private collection

Plate 66
Britain
Silver Teapot, Staffordshire ware,
c. 1790
Glazed earthenware with on-glaze
luster
6 inches high
Everson Museum of Art, Syracuse,
New York

These teapots, known as "poor
man's Sheffield," were ceramic imitations of the silver teapots used
by wealthier tea drinkers.

oddity from the 1930s and 1940s, the American spirit of invention did not enliven teapot design until the 1960s. Late in the decade the noted Funk artist, Robert Arneson, worked on a series of teapots, primarily as a vulgarly satiric device. *A Social Gathering for the Late Afternoon* (1969), in which the word "Tea" creates the spout and the handle of the lid, is one of his more gentle works and lightly spoofs the ritual of tea (Plate 65). But Arneson's treatment of other tea-pots is more deliberately offensive. Aggressive, anatomically detailed phallic spouts, pubic hair, and vaginal openings give his teapots a disturb-ing, comic-serious sexual presence. Arneson influenced an entire generation of ceramists and encouraged a satiric and provocative approach to ceramics and its traditional forms.

Richard Shaw, a student of Arneson's, con-tributed a very different approach to the visceral character of Funk, one that deals with the de-ception of the eye. His teapots continue the tra-dition of trompe l'oeil surface imitations that was begun by the Yixing potters in the sixteenth cen-tury. Shaw chooses subjects with a sense of irony, as we see in *Cardboard Tea Service* from 1975 (Plate 95). His influence during the 1970s was immense, releasing a flood of ceramic *faux* through the decade and into the 1980s.

This interest in clay's ability to mimic other materials is by no means new, a point demon-strated by an early Yixing teapot covered in real-istic nuts and fruit (Plate 122). And in the eighteenth century Staffordshire teapots with sil-ver luster overglaze were sold as "poor man's Sheffield" to those who could not afford real sil-ver teapots (Plate 66). Marble, gold, wood, and others materials were also imitated.

The enduring influence of both Yixing and trompe l'oeil can also be seen in the work of Rich-ard Notkin, an Arneson student and one of the most intriguing teapot makers of our time. The manner in which Yixing potters and Chinese scholars were able to infuse a sensually beautiful object with symbolic and intellectual content has fascinated Notkin. He has reproduced the distinctive Yixing clays, added some variations of his own, and adopted a series of tough issues as his subject matter: the fear of death, urban blight, the hostage crisis of 1981, the dangers of nuclear energy.

The latter concern was explored in the *Cool-ing Towers* series (Plate 86), which was inspired thematically by the near-miss of the Three Mile Island nuclear failure and formally by a Yixing teapot of two bound boxes (Plate 85). Notkin con-verted the Yixing boxes into a pair of cooling tower shapes that have a sinister elegance. The sight of hot steaming tea pouring out of one of these objects should be enough to unsettle even the most ardent pro-nuclear advocate. In other vari-ations on this theme he has included surrealistic telephone poles as handles, images that came from a U.S. Army film on nuclear tests that showed buildings, poles, and trees distorting into Daliesque shapes during an atomic blast.

There has been, of course, a tradition of po-litical imagery in teapot-making, including a group of portrait teapots of prominent figures in British politics produced around 1900 by Foley Pottery under the name of *Intarsio* (Plates 99, 100), as well as an unflattering commercial teapot of an arrogant Margaret Thatcher. But Notkin's work goes much further than any of these, most of which draw the line at simple caricature. In his *Heartfelt* series, each teapot, based on a disturb-ingly real heart shape, has been conceived as a small but moving monument to man's inhuman-ity to man. The heart image functions on many levels, ironically symbolizing human emotion, compassion, and conscience and, at the same

time, our individual vulnerability. In *Hostage* (1987) the "heart" is painfully bound in chains (Plate 87). Other heart teapots deal with South Africa, Afghanistan, Vietnam, and Hiroshima. As the critics Sarah Bodine and Michael Dunas commented in an article in *American Ceramics* from 1987, "In the Lilliputian theatre of the minature, where scale is the allegory of power . . . Notkin uses the table top to narrate the complexity and magnitude of society's actions."

It is the very familiarity of the teapot that gives Notkin's work much of its edge, luring observers with its comforting intimacy before confronting

them with a powerful and often painful message. Working with issues of human pain on a more personal level, Anne Kraus employs a similar device. Her narrative teapots tell tales of humiliating rejection, of dashed hopes and lost love (Plates 5, 6). Lulled at first by the patterns and images that constitute Kraus's highly decorative style, the viewer only later discovers the intensity and painfulness of the artist's message. *Los Angeles Times* critic Colin Gardner sees these pots as "stages for lovelorn, anxious scenarios and texts . . . a hermetic world that evokes repressive Victorianism, where taking tea or arranging flowers in a vase

Plate 67
The Mad Hatter's tea party, by John Tenniel, from *Alice's Adventures in Wonderland*.

becomes ritualistic escapes from the rather barren torment of brooding loneliness and despair."

Turning our discussion now to twentieth-century Britain, we find that a rather different attitude has characterized that country's ceramic artists. British ceramists have tended to avoid political and uncomfortably emotional issues, generally preferring to approach the teapot from a more objective, formalist point of view. A tradition of humorous pots has also thrived. The British ceramic industry produced a large series of amusing teapots during the 1920s and 1930s in the forms of cars, trains, tanks, the old woman who lived in a shoe, Humpty-Dumpty, houses, boats, and cats (p. 3 and Plates 13, 14, 17). These charming, industrially made folk wares were extensively imitated in Japan.

In the past few decades some British ceramists have begun to address complex thematic issues through the teapot, among them Carol McNicol, whose delightfully surreal *Alice in Wonderland Tea Set* (1971–72) challenges the notion of functionality (Plate 68). Anthony Bennett, arguably one of the finest modelers working in England today, has been influenced by two apparently dissimilar sources. *Dinosaurs Pointing*

Plate 68
Carol McNicol, Britain
Alice in Wonderland Tea Set,
1971–72
Glazed earthenware
7 inches high
Private collection

This piece was inspired by the Mad Hatter's tea party. As Alice was leaving she glanced back at the guests; in the words of the story, "the last time she saw them they were trying to put the Dormouse into the teapot."

(1981), a pair of well-endowed teapots and one of his masterpieces, has been inspired by the style of the underground comics (Plate 74), while the *Frog/Fossil* series from 1983 refers to the realm of natural history (p. 5).

But these artists are atypical; to a greater extent the British teapot is approached from a safer, designerly, formalist viewpoint. One of the country's strongest contributions to contemporary ceramics has been the emergence of a strong "pictorialism" in the 1970s and 1980s, which deals with form as though it were actually a drawing. Elizabeth Fritsch initiated this style in the early 1970s. Her extraordinary pots were actually narrow and flat, but by creating false perspectives Fritsch was able to convey the illusion of the pots as full-bodied, voluptuous volumes.

This pictorialism has found particularly sophisticated expression in the work of Linda Gunn-Russell and Nicholas Homoky. Gunn-Russell's teapots are a stylish tease between three and two dimensions, playing with line and perspective as though the teapot were being created with pen and paper rather than with clay and glaze (Plate 35). Homoky, on the other hand, creates reductive, abstracted teapot shapes, sometimes with lids and sometimes without. His forms function primarily as surfaces on which to draw teapot shapes. Created in stark white porcelain with inlaid black drawings, the teapots are impressive and primarily graphic in their impact (Plate 33).

The use of the teapot or tea service as a three dimensional still life is an extension of this pictorialism, the inspiration of which comes mainly from modern painting. The cup sculptures of Roy Lichtenstein in the late 1960s, for instance, dealt brilliantly with this notion and he has recently created a teapot in a similar Pop spirit (Plate 34).

While some teapots illustrated here reveal little interest in the history of the form, others are engaged in an active dialogue with teapots of the past. The act of taking aesthetic sustenance from art history has had the effect recently of turning the entire history of fine and decorative art into a giant bin of ideas, images, and techniques from which the artist can freely quote. At its worst this pluralism has produced mundane imitation. But at its best it has created exceptionally literate art that treats history as assemblage, rich with social commentary and wry satiric perspectives.

Adrian Saxe's *French Curve* and *Ampersand* teapots from 1987 are an example of this approach at its finest (Plates 133, 135). These teapots stand as a complex homage to the sensuality and extravagance of eighteenth-century European court porcelains, on the one hand. On the other, they respond to the humor and eccentricity of the nineteenth-century Chinese *famille verte* character tea and wine pots (Plate 134). Saxe views court porcelains less as decorative bibelots than as invocations of power and prestige. While he does embrace the material tradition of lush glazes and fired gold and silver surfaces, he also satirizes them, questioning materialism and the politics of elitism with which the court porcelains are associated. Because Saxe's pots both pander to and question the viewer's attraction to their seductive surfaces, critic Peter Schjeldahl describes Saxe's brilliant pots as "glamorous and untrustworthy, like a pedigreed dog that has been known to bite."

The teapot with its complex assemblage of elements has also proven to be a source of inspiration to architecturally inspired designers working in the Post-Modern style. Los Angeles-based Peter Shire became an early exponent of the movement and one of the first American designers to work with Milan's Memphis design group. Although he now works primarily in furniture and sculpture, Shire made his name as a ceramist with a particular fascination for the teapot form. His *Scorpion Teapot* (1984) is one of the classics of this genre, taking the basic geometry of the Malevich teapot and replacing its reductivism and conceptualism with a playful geometry that is part Art Deco, part Constructivism, and part Futurism (Plate 11).

The investigation of the teapot as an art form has reached an inventive peak in the past two decades but the exploration is by no means over. Indeed the long love affair with this modestly scaled, spouted vessel shows no sign of abating. Our enduring fascination with the form grows from the intriguing interplay of familiarity and complexity. But the teapot also evokes deeply sensual feelings and memories. It resonates with the misty warmth of family gatherings redolent with the fragrances not just of tea but of glowing fireplaces, freshly baked scones, and damp afternoons.

This eccentric collection of teapots embraces the ceremonial connotations of the teapot but it also veers off at oblique angles from the conventional role of the teapot to explore unexpected zones of creativity. Collectively these objects comprise a three-dimensional entertainment, a colorfully costumed pantomime around the theme of the teapot. In common with pantomime they tend towards an overstated theatricality and a joyful sense of parody. Elevating the banal through their eccentric vision, these teapots have moments of melodrama, hilarity, and camp, but also of ringing profundity and tenderness.

Plate 69
Minton, Ltd., Britain
Cock and Monkey Teapot,
Majolica ware, c. 1880
Glazed earthenware
6 inches high
Private collection

Plate 70
Modeled by J. J. Kandler, Germany
Produced by Meissen Porcelain
Works, Germany
Cock and Hen Teapot, c. 1740
Glazed porcelain with on-glaze
decoration
6½ inches high
Christie's, London

Plate 71
Britain
Camel with Howdah, Staffordshire
ware salt glaze, c. 1745
Salt-glazed stoneware
7¾ inches high
Victoria and Albert Museum,
London

Plate 72
Edward Bingham, Britain
Produced by Castle Hedinghan
Pottery, Britain
Figurative Teapot, 1988
Lead-glazed earthenware with slips
10½ inches high
Victoria and Albert Museum, London

This teapot was created by one of
England's most eccentric rustic
potters. Its inspiration came from
a similar but more sophisticated
Meissen piece from 1712.

Plate 73
Moore Brothers Pottery, Britain
Camel Teapot, c. 1875
Ruby-glazed earthenware
8 inches high
Victoria and Albert Museum,
London

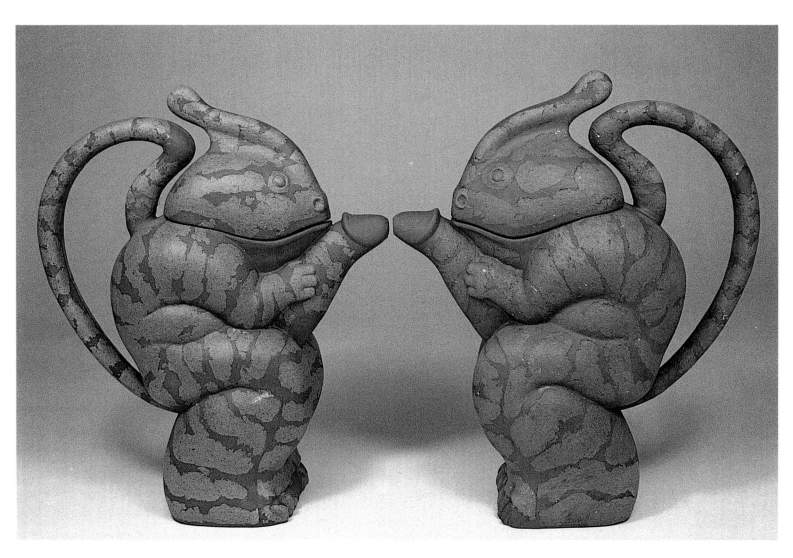

Plate 74
Anthony Bennett, Britain
Dinosaurs Pointing, 1981
Glazed earthenware
9½ inches high
Private collection

Plate 75
Charles Brannam, Britain
Dragon Teapot, Barum ware,
c. 1885
Glazed earthenware with slips
4¾ inches high
Collection of Betty Asher

Plate 76
Martin Brothers, Britain
Grotesque Teapot, c. 1898
Salt-glazed stoneware
5½ inches high
Private collection

Wallace Martin, who modeled this
teapot, worked in his youth as a
stonemason on the Houses of Parliament, roughing out neo-Gothic
gargoyles and acquiring a taste for
the grotesque that remained with
him throughout his career.

Plate 77
Modeled by J. J. Kandler, Germany
Produced by Meissen Porcelain
Works, Germany
Monkey Teapot, c. 1735
Glazed porcelain with on-glaze
decoration
7 1/2 inches high
The Metropolitan Museum of Art,
New York, gift of Irwin Untermeyer

Plate 78
Minton, Ltd., Britain
Monkey Teapot, Majolica ware,
c. 1880
Glazed earthenware
6 inches high
Private collection

Plate 79
Lidya Buzio, United States
Soho Roofscape Teapot, 1983
Burnished earthenware with
overglaze
5 inches high
Collection of Betty Asher

Buzio paints cityscapes on her sensual burnished vessels, here using
the volume of the teapot to suggest
an encapsuled view of Manhattan's
Soho with its Italianate rooflines.

Plate 80
Clarice Cliff, Britain
Produced by Newport Pottery,
Britain
Teepee Teapot, c. 1950
Glazed earthenware
5⅞ inches high
Sotheby's, London

This postwar piece, designed spe-
cifically for the Canadian market,
reads "Greetings from Canada"
on the base.

Plate 81
Mabel Lucie Attwell, Britain
Produced by Foley Pottery, Britain
Nursery Teapot, 1926
Glazed earthenware
5 inches high
Private collection

Attwell was a popular illustrator of children's books during the early decades of this century. A number of nursery tea sets like this one appeared in the 1920s, reflecting an interest in tea novelties rather than a rise in serious tea drinking among the occupants of England's nurseries.

Plate 82
Jerry Berta, United States
Diner Teapot, 1986
Glazed earthenware
7 inches high
Private collection

Berta's fascination with 1950s greasy spoons has extended to his pottery and gallery, which he has created from a converted classic 1950s roadside diner.

Plate 83
Britain
House Teapot, Staffordshire ware
salt glaze, c. 1745
Salt-glazed stoneware
5½ inches high
Victoria and Albert Museum,
London

Plate 84
Stanley Tygerman and Margaret
McCurry, United States
Tygerman Teaside Teaset, 1986
Glazed porcelain
10 inches high
Swid Powell Design, New York

———

Architects from Michael Graves to
Robert Venturi have recently begun
to enter the field of ceramic design. The results have been un-
even but this service by Tygerman
and McCurry charmingly explores
the architecture of the teapot by
updating the classic eighteenth-
century house teapot.

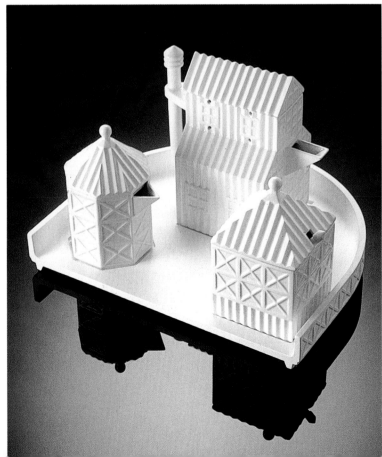

75

Plate 85
China
Wrapped Boxes, Yixing ware,
Tua-Kwang period, 1821–50
Stoneware
8½ inches wide
Collection of Emily Fisher Landau

Plate 86
Richard Notkin, United States
Cooling Towers Teapot #1, Yixing
Series, 1983
Stoneware
6½ inches high
Collection of Betty Asher

This teapot was inspired by a
Yixing teapot consisting of two
boxes wrapped together. When
filled with hot tea it provides a
chilling commentary on the dangers of nuclear energy.

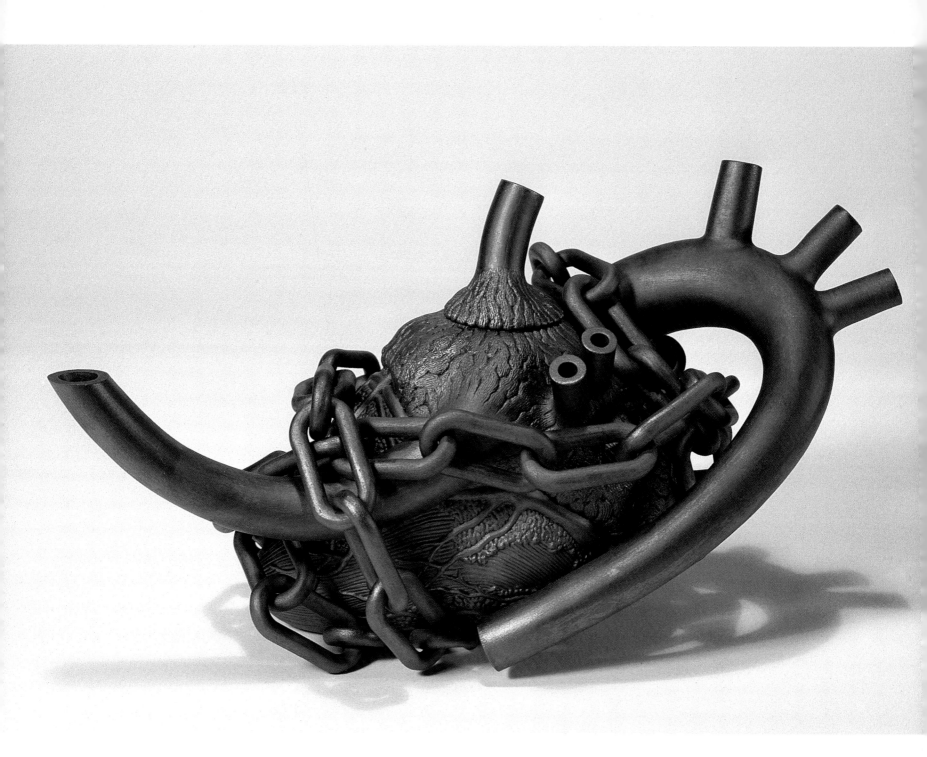

Plate 87
Richard Notkin, United States
Hostage Teapot, Yixing series, 1987
Stoneware
5 inches high
Collection of Gloria and
Sonny Kamm

———

In an ironic twist on the conventional symbolism of compassion, Notkin's teapots stand as small monuments symbolizing man's inhumanity to man.

Plate 88
Clayton Bailey, United States
Robot Teapot, 1979
Glazed earthenware
7½ inches high
Collection of Betty Asher

Plate 89
Steven Montgomery, United States
Sherman Teapot, 1985
Earthenware, paint, glaze
8⅛ inches high
Collection of Daniel Jacobs

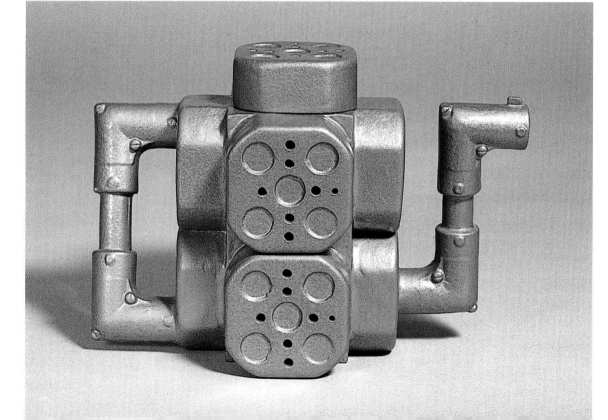

Plate 90
Shin-Ta-Pin, China
Wrapped Teapot, Yixing ware,
c. 1645
Stoneware
3 inches high
Collection of Emily Fisher Landau

This teapot was created in imitation
of a square seal or stamp that has
been wrapped in cloth.

Plate 91
J. Bethal, United States
Wrapped Teapot, c. 1982
Glazed earthenware, china paint
11¼ inches high
Collection of Betty Asher

Plate 92
Carol James, Britain
Plumbing Teapot, 1973
Glazed earthenware
6 inches high
Private collection

Plate 93
Carol James, Britain
Sink Teapot, 1973
Glazed earthenware
5 inches high
Private collection

Plate 94
Richard Notkin, United States
Oval Curbside Teapot (Variation # 7), Yixing Series, 1986
Stoneware
3⅞ inches high
Private collection

This teapot, inspired by Yixing wares, expresses the artist's concerns about urban decay and the dilemma of homelessness in America, symbolized by the undernourished dog.

Plate 95
Richard Shaw, United States
Cardboard Tea Service, 1975
Glazed porcelain, ceramic decals
7 inches high
Private collection

Plate 96
Leopold Foulem, Canada
Thière, 1987
Ceramic, wire
6 inches high
Collection of the artist

The teapot was formed by dipping a wire-mesh shape into slip and firing the clay-coated wire in a kiln. The wire fired away in the kiln creates a revealing and deli- cate teapot with an ironic sense of interior, exterior, and defeated purpose.

Plate 97
Jan Axel, United States
Victoria Teapot, 1977
Glazed porcelain, luster
15 inches high
Private collection

Plate 98
John Revelry, United States
Kentucky Fried Teapot, 1979
Glazed earthenware
5 inches high
Collection of Betty Asher

———

Colonel Sanders, the legendary
founder of the Kentucky Fried
Chicken chain, is the subject of
this somewhat macabre portrait
teapot.

Plate 99
Foley Pottery, Britain
President Paul Kruger, Intarsio
ware, c. 1900
Glazed earthenware
5 inches high
Private collection
———
This portrait of "Oom Paul," the
president of the Transvaal Republic
(against which Britain waged the
Second Boer War), is one of a
series of the Foley Pottery's por-
traits of turn-of-the-century political
figures.

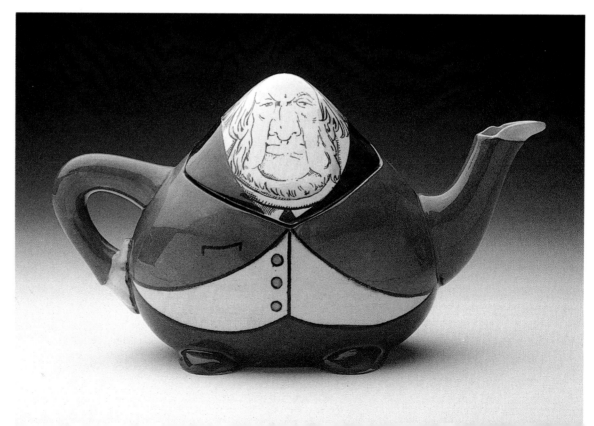

Plate 100
Foley Pottery, Britain
Prime Minister William Gladstone,
Intarsio ware, c. 1900
Glazed earthenware
5 inches high
Private collection

Plate 101
Anthony Bennett, Britain
Teddy Roosevelt Teapot, 1986
Glazed earthenware
11 inches high
Private collection

Plate 102
Worcester Porcelain Company, Britain
Aesthetic Teapot (Oscar Wilde),
c. 1881
Glazed porcelain
6 inches high
Dyson Perrins Museum,
Worcester, Massachusetts

The base of this teapot is inscribed
with a parody of Oscar Wilde's
famous epigram, which reads,
"Fearful consequences through the
laws of natural selection and evolution of living up to one's teapot." One side shows Wilde as a
man and the other as a woman.

Plate 103
Exile Ceramics, Britain
Queen Elizabeth with Corgi Spout, c. 1980
Glazed ceramic
11 inches high
Collection of Betty Asher

Plate 104
John de Fazio, United States
Brooke Shields, 1986–87
Glazed ceramic
12 inches high
Collection of Sanford Besser

Plate 105
Viola Frey, United States
Untitled, 1975–76
Earthenware with slips and china paint
14 inches high
Collection of Betty Asher

This teapot is an assemblage of junk figurines and ceramic ornaments that the artist has collected from flea markets. These elements are molded, cut, assembled, and painted with slips and china paint.

Plate 106
Jeannot Blackburn, Canada
Bride Teapot, 1987
Glazed earthenware
10 inches high
Private collection

Plate 107
Tim Mitchinson, Britain
Produced by Topor Pottery, Britain
Vampire Teapot, 1984
Glazed earthenware
11 inches high
Private collection

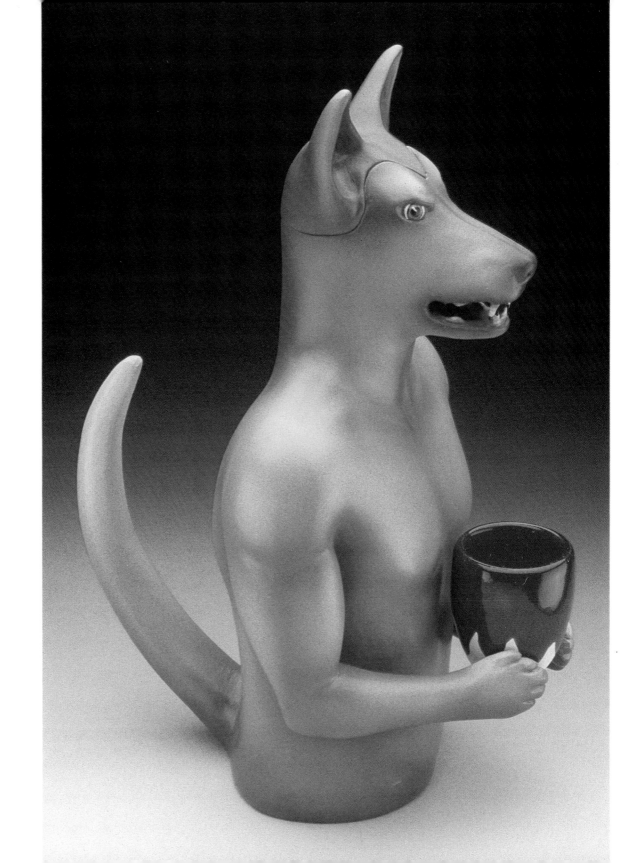

Plate 108
Jack Thompson, United States
Garth Clark Editions
*Werewolf Teapot with Sang de
Boeuf Cup*, 1984
Earthenware and acrylic paint
8¾ inches high
Collection of Betty Asher

Plate 109
Mark Burns, United States
Garth Clark Editions
X-Ray Teapot, 1984
Painted earthenware
9 inches high
Collection of Sandford Besser

This distinctively punk-inspired teapot is decorated with representa-
tions of small dental X-ray sheets.

Plate 110
Richard Notkin, United States
Skull Teapot, 1981
Stoneware
6 inches high
Collection of Betty Asher

Notkin's skull is not intended to be ghoulish but rather to evoke the idea of the skull as a "container" for the brain and therefore the seat of human conscience.

Plate 111
Adrian Saxe, United States
Untitled, 1973
Copper-red glazed porcelain
9 inches high
Private collection

Plate 112
Akio Takamori, United States
Teapot with Figures, 1987
Glazed porcelain, china paint
6½ inches high
Collection of Betty Asher

Takamori is inspired by the sensuality of pouring liquids in his erotic explorations of the vessel.

Plate 113
Johann G. Kirchner, Germany
Produced by Meissen Porcelain
Works, Germany
Figurative Teapot, c. 1725
Glazed porcelain with on-glaze
decoration
6 inches high
The Metropolitan Museum of Art,
New York, gift of Irwin Untermeyer

Plate 114
Beatrice Wood, United States
Woman Teapot, 1984
Luster-glazed earthenware
10 inches high
Collection of Betty Asher

The lustrous surface here is created by firing in an oxygen-starved atmosphere, a process that brings the metallic salts in the glaze to the surface and creates a distinctive iridescence.

Plate 115
Doulton and Watts, Britain
Seated Man Teapot, c. 1840
Salt-glazed stoneware
9½ inches high
Private collection

Plate 116
Anne Kraus, United States
Michael and Edna Teapot, 1987
Glazed whiteware
8 inches high
Collection of Karel Reisz

This teapot captures a moment of domestic tension as the figure of Edna flees from the room. The fat, rounded volume of the teapot is treated by the artist as though it were a fish-eye lens, capturing deep perspectives within a circular format.

Plate 117
Katherine McBride, United States
Tea Cozy, 1986
Porcelain
10 inches high
Dorothy Weiss Gallery,
San Francisco

The quiet contentment of late afternoon teatime at home is captured in this complex and romantic teapot. Inset shows reverse view.

Plate 118
Serge Bohagisao and Agnes
Decoux, France
Baby Teapot, c. 1982
Glazed earthenware
4½ inches high
Collection of Betty Asher

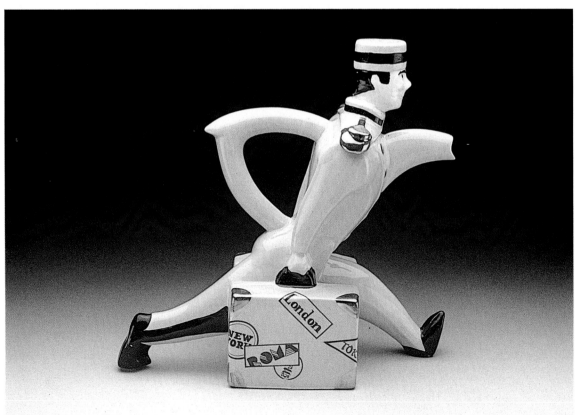

Plate 119
Martin Bibby, Britain
Produced by Swineside Ceramics,
Britain
Bellhop Teapot, 1985
Glazed ceramic
12 inches high
Private collection

Plate 120
Danka Napriokowska, Britain
Walking Tea Service, 1973–74
Glazed earthenware
7½ inches high
Private collection

Napriokowska first produced this
service in limited quantities from
her small pottery but became tired
of "painting plaid socks" and sold
the design to industry.

Plate 121
China
Prune Branch Teapot,
Yixing ware, Kwang-Hsu period,
1875–1908
Stoneware
7½ inches high
Collection of Emily Fisher Landau

Plate 122
Li-Shan, China
Pomegranate Teapot, Yixing ware,
Tua-Kwang period, 1821–50
Stoneware
5¼ inches high
Collection of Emily Fisher Landau

———

The pomegranate teapot with its
attached fruits and nuts symbolized fecundity, the blessing of numerous offspring for the owner.

Plate 123
Sun Hung Sin, China
Plum Flower Teapot, Yixing ware,
Yung-Cheng period, 1723–35
Stoneware
4¼ inches high
Collection of Emily Fisher Landau

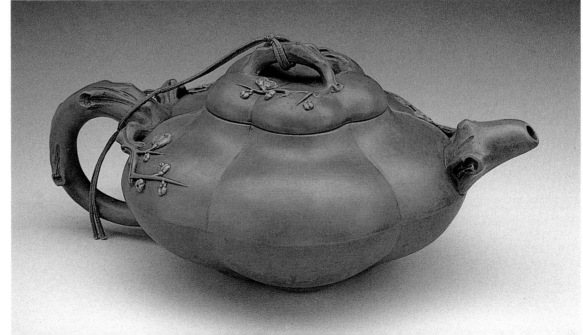

Plate 124
Britain
Bamboo Teapot, Staffordshire ware,
1770
Glazed earthenware
5 inches high
Victoria and Albert Museum,
London

———

Yixing teapots had a major impact
in the design of European tea
wares throughout the eighteenth
century. This teapot is a Western
interpretation of the Yixing bamboo teapot.

Plate 125
China
Bamboo Bundle Teapot, Yixing
ware, Yung-Cheng period, 1723–35
Stoneware
3⅝ inches high
Collection of Emily Fisher Landau

Plate 126
Minton, Ltd., Britain
Gourd Teapot, Majolica ware,
c. 1880
Glazed earthenware
4¾ inches high
Private collection

Plate 127
Rozenburg Plateelfabriek,
Netherlands
Tea Service, 1903
Glazed earthenware
6 inches to 4 inches high
Rijksmuseum, Amsterdam
___
Although this ware was popularly
known as eggshell porcelain be-
cause of its delicate, thin walls, the
clay was actually closer to a white
earthenware.

Plate 128
Coalport Pottery, Britain
Tea Service, c. 1820
Glazed porcelain
4 inches to 8¼ inches high
Victoria and Albert Museum,
London

Plate 129
Lynn Turner, United States
Tea Service IV-4, 1980
Porcelain, stains
6 inches high
Private collection

Plate 130
Whieldon/Wedgwood, Britain
Pineapple Teapot, c. 1765
Glazed earthenware
5 inches high
Everson Museum of Art, Syracuse,
New York

Plate 131
Whieldon/Wedgwood, Britain
Cabbage Teapot, c. 1765
Glazed earthenware
4½ inches high
Everson Museum of Art, Syracuse,
New York

Plate 132
Adrian Saxe, United States
Gourd Teapot, 1982
Porcelain
3¾ inches high
Collection of Aaron Milrad

Plate 133
Adrian Saxe, United States
French Curve Teapot, 1987
Glazed porcelain, stoneware,
overglaze
11½ inches high
Private collection

Inset:
Plate 134
China
Pair of Character Teapots/Wine Vessels, famille verte ware, c. 1880
Glazed porcelain
8 inches high
Collection of Connie and Adrian Saxe

These pots take the shape of the Chinese Wu character, which means prosperity.

Plate 135
Adrian Saxe, United States
Ampersand Teapot, 1987
Glazed porcelain, overglaze
10½ inches high
Private collection

BIBLIOGRAPHY

Bartholomew, Therese Tse. *I-Hsing Wares.* New York: China Institute of America, 1977.

Foley, Tricia. *Having Tea.* New York: Clarkson N. Potter, 1987.

Okakura, Kakuzo. *The Book of Tea.* 1906. Reprint. New York: Dover Press, 1964. (The original was published by Fox, Duffield and Company in 1906. The Dover edition includes an introduction by E. F. Bleiler that corrects some of the errors and misspellings in the original printing.)

Simpson, Helen. *The London Ritz Book of Afternoon Tea: The Art and Pleasure of Taking Afternoon Tea.* London: Ebury Press, 1986.

Soshitsu, Sen XV. *Tea Life, Tea Mind.* New York: John Weatherhill, 1979.

Street-Porter, Janet, and Tim Street-Porter. *The British Teapot.* London: Angus and Robertson, 1981.

Ukers, William H. *All About Tea.* New York: Trade Journal Company, 1935.

Plate 136
Coille Hooven, United States
Teapot with Lid, 1978
Glazed porcelain
7 1/4 inches high
Oakland Museum, Oakland,
California

ACKNOWLEDGMENTS

The author would like to thank David McFadden of the Cooper-Hewitt Museum; Paul Greenhalgh at Christie's, London; Robert Woolley and Tish Roberts at Sotheby's, New York; Oliver Watson of the Victoria and Albert Museum, London; Therese Tse Bartholomew of the Asian Art Museum, San Francisco; Patty Dean of the Arkansas Art Center, Little Rock; Barbara Perry of the Everson Museum of Art, Syracuse, New York; Harry Frost of the Dyson Perrins Museum, Worcester, Massachusetts; Brian Haughton of Brian Haughton Antiques, London; and Richard Nicholas of the Tea House, London. I would also like to extend thanks to many collectors for allowing me access to their homes and their belongings. I am particularly grateful for the generous cooperation of Betty Asher, Sanford Besser, and Emily Fisher Landau.

In regard to this book's actual creation, I am indebted to John White and Tony Cunha for their excellent photography. Wayne Kuwada and Mark Del Vecchio have, as usual, given me considerable support on an organizational level, and Gretchen Atkins cast a welcome weather eye over the manuscript. Above all, I would like to thank Sharon Gallagher of Abbeville Press for her support and cheerful encouragement. The lively design by Julie Rauer and the sensitive editing of Constance Herndon have brought it to life.

In writing and assembling this book I have drawn inspiration from several sources, notably Kakuzo Okakura's classic, *The Book of Tea* (1906), and more recently Helen Simpson's delightful and evocative *The London Ritz Book of Afternoon Tea* (1986). Other works that I have drawn from are listed in the bibliography.

Finally, I would like to dedicate this book to teapot collectors, tea drinkers, and eccentrics everywhere.

GRC

Plate 137
The tea service shown in this early twentieth-century photograph includes a teapot rather than the tea bowl traditionally used in the formal Japanese tea ceremony.

INDEX

PHOTOGRAPHY CREDITS

The photographers and the sources of the photographic material other than those indicated in the captions are as follows:

Arkansas Art Center, Little Rock, Arkansas: plates 104, 109; Jan Axel, plate 96; Glen Baxter: plate 45; Anthony Bennet: plate 74; Jerry Berta: back cover/plate 82; Bettmann Archive/BBC Hulton: endpapers, plates 18, 25, 37, 43, 44; Jeannot Blackburn: plate 106; Garth Clark: plates 20, 26, 57, 59, 61, 62, 66, 76, 81, 92, 93; Cooper-Hewitt Museum, New York, the Smithsonian Institution's National Museum of Design: plates 55, 63; Tony Cunha: back cover/plate 69, plates 5, 7, 8, 9, 23, 33, 34, 50, 52, 53, 75, 78, 79, 86, 87, 88, 91, 98, 99, 100, 103, 105, 107, 108, 110, 112, 114, 115, 116, 118, 126, 134; Kim Dicky: plate 54; Michael Duvall: plate 10; M. Lee Fathersee: plate 136; Ferrin Gallery at Pinch Pottery, Northampton, Massachusetts: plates 21, 32, 120; Leopold Foulem: plate 96; Courtney Frisse: plates 130, 131; Nancy Hirsch: backcover/plate 132; Mike Johns: plate 51; Cindy Kolodziejski: page 4; James Lawton: plate 49; Colin C. McRae: plate 129; Michaelson/Orient Gallery, London: plate 35; Steven Montgomery: plate 89; New York Public Library, New York: plates 31, 39; Richard Notkin: plate 94; Pierpoint Morgan Library, New York, Houghton Collection: plate 67; Rijksmuseum, Amsterdam: plate 127; Royal College of Art, London: page 2, plate 68; Amy Sabrina: plate 4; Esther Saks Gallery, Chicago: plate 36; Adrian Saxe: plate 111; Joe Schopplein: plate 95; Eric Shambroom, plate 138; Peter Shire: plate 11; R. Twinings and Company, Ltd.: plate 42; John White: cover/plate 119, pages 3, 5, plates 2, 3, 6, 13, 14, 17, 38, 47, 85, 90, 101, 121, 122, 123, 125, 133, 135

Plate 138
Jill Crowley, Britain
Untitled, 1970
Raku
6¼ inches high
Collection of Daniel Jacobs